EDITOR: JONAH LAYMAN

עם ישראל וארץ ישראל

THE PEOPLE AND ITS LAND
SIMCHA KLING

UNITED SYNAGOGUE OF AMERICA/DEPARTMENT OF YOUTH ACTIVITES

UNITED SYNAGOGUE OF AMERICA
DEPARTMENT OF YOUTH ACTIVITIES

Rabbi Paul Freedman, *Director*
Jules A. Gutin, *Assistant Director*
Mirjam Mundstzuk-Ohrbach, *Projects Director*
Elliot Forcheimer, *Activities Director*
Martin S. Kunoff, *Activities Administrator*
Daniel B. Ripps, *Kadima Director*
Amy Katz Wasser, *Projects Coordinator*
Yitzchak Jacobsen, *Director, Israel Office*
Shimon Lipsky, *Nativ Director*
Hezki Arieli, *Central Shaliach*
Jonah Layman, *Educational Consultant*

INTERNATIONAL YOUTH COMMISSION

Jeremy J. Fingerman, *Co-Chairman*
Stephen S. Wolnek, *Co-Chairman*

UNITED SYNAGOGUE OF AMERICA

Franklin D. Kreutzer, *President*
Rabbi Benjamin Z. Kreitman, *Executive Vice President*
Rabbi Jerome M. Epstein, *Senior Vice President Chief Executive Officer*
Jack Mittleman, *Administrative Vice President*

A publication of the National Youth Commission, United Synagogue of America.
155 Fifth Avenue, New York, New York 10010.

Manufactured in the United States of America.
Typography and lithography by Star Composition, Inc.
Cover design by Amir Zeltser.

Library of Congress Catalog Card Number: 88-050584

Copyright © 1988, United Synagogue Youth.

WORLD ZIONIST ORGANIZATION

Office of the Chairman of the Executive

May 16, 1988

Rabbi Paul Freedman
Department of Youth Activities
The United Synagogue of America
155 Fifth Avenue,
New York, NY 10010
USA

Dear Rabbi Freedman:

I am pleased to send warmest greetings from Jerusalem to the members of the United Synagogue of America and the United Synagogue Youth movement on the occasion of the publication of your sourcebook related to Am Yisrael ve-Eretz Yisrael -- The People and Its Land.

The United Synagogue of America that is currently celebrating its seventy-fifth anniversary has forged strong ties with the State of Israel through the longstanding commitment of the Mesorati (Conservative) Movement to Zionism. Particularly encouraging is your emphasis on youth and the link with Israel and her people through the significant work of the United Synagogue Youth and your Israel-oriented programs that have won the admiration of the various departments of the World Zionist Organization.

Rabbi Simcha Kling deserves to be commended for the fine selection of articles in this year's sourcebook that traces the attachment of the Jewish people to the Land of Israel from the Biblical period to our present times. I hope that those who have the opportunity to read this commendable effort will find it an invariable source of information that will encourage more youth, and adults too, to share in the growth and advancement of the Jewish State.

Sincerely yours,

Simcha Dinitz
Chairman

Jerusalem 91920, P.O.B. 92, Telephone: 02-202222, Telex: 25236, Fax.: 224533, Cables: Zionit

FOREIGN AFFAIRS AND DEFENCE COMMITTEE
THE CHAIRMAN

ועדת החוץ והבטחון
היושב-ראש

הכנסת
THE KNESSET
JERUSALEM

May 29, 1988

Rabbi Paul Freedman
Director
The United Synagogue of America
155 Fifth Avenue
New York, N.Y. 10010
U. S. A.

Dear Rabbi Freedman,

Thank you for your letter of April 28th.

Following is my suggested letter of introduction:

Dear Friend,

I have heard with pleasure of the intention of the
Conservative (Mesorati) Synagogues to publish a year book on
the subject: "AM YISRAEL VE-ERETZ ISRAEL - My People and Its
Land."

I greatly admire the Conservative (Mesorati) movement which
has been unsurpassed in its devotion to the central
interests of the Jewish people and particularly, to the
State of Israel.

Rabbi Simcha Kling is a notable scholar with a deep insight
into the spirit of Jewish history, and I am sure that all
readers of the Yearbook, including its young readers, will
benefit greatly from his interpretation of our national and
religious experience.

Warm regards,

Abba Eban

D18-135

ACKNOWLEDGMENTS

Chapter I:

Translations from *The Torah*. *The Prophets*, and *The Writings*. Published by the Jewish Publication Society (JPS), Philadelphia, 1962, 1978, 1982.

Chapter III:

Translations from *Sim Shalom* edited by Rabbi Jules Harlow. Published by the Rabbinical Assembly and the United Synagogue of America, New York, 1983. (Also utilized in Chapter IV.)

Judaism by Israel Levinthal. Published by Funk & Wagnalls, New York, 1935. pp. 249-250.

Chapter IV

Studies in Judaism by Solomon Schechter. First Series published by JPS, Philadelphia, 1896. pp. 85, 108, 109-110. Second Series published by JPS, Philadelphia, 1908. p. 202.

A Treasury of Jewish Letters by Franz Kobler. Published by Farrar, Straus, and Young, New York, 1952. Vol. 1, p. 242; Vol. II, pp. 305-309, 483-484.

Out of Our People's Past by Walter Ackerman. Published by the United Synagogue Commission on Jewish Education, New York, 1977. p. 39.

Rabbi Nachman's Wisdom translated by Aryeh Kaplan. Published in Brooklyn, NY, 1973. pp. 37, 93.

Rabbi Meir of Rothenberg by Irving A. Agus. Published by Dropsie College for Hebrew and Cognate Learning, Philadelphia, 1947. p. 681.

Chapter V

Edmond de Rothschild by Isaac Naiditch. Published by the Zionist Organization of America, Washington, D.C., 1945. pp. 22-23.

Chapter VI

The Zionist Idea by Arthur Hertzberg. Published by Doubleday, Garden City, NY, 1959. pp. 105, 111-112, 145, 151, 153, 402, 419. (Also utilized in Chapter VII, pp. 262, 267).

Banner of Jerusalem by Jacob Agus. Published by Bloch Publishing Co., New York, 1946. p. 69.

Chapter VII

A Jewish State by Theodore Herzl, translated by Jacob de Haas. Published by the Federation of American Zionists, New York, 1917. Portions of the preface.

Theodore Herzl by Alex Bein, translated by Maurice Samuel. Published by JPS, Philadelphia, 1940, p. 239.

Max Nordau to His People by Max Nordau. Published by Scopus Publishing Co., New York, 1941. pp. 117, 188.

An Answer to Ernest Bevin by Vladimir Jabotinsky. Published in New York, 1946.

The Letters and Papers of Chaim Weizmann by Chaim Weizmann. Published by Oxford University Press, London, 1968. Vol. I, pp. 36-37.

Memoirs of David Ben-Gurion compiled by Thomas R. Bransten. Published by World Publishing Co., New York, 1970. p. 34.

Rebirth and Destiny of Israel by David Ben-Gurion, translated by Mordekhai Nurock. Published by the New York Philosophical Library, NY, 1954. pp. 4, 37, 174-175.

"Martin Buber's Impact on German Zionism before World War I" by Jehuda Reinharz in *Studies in Zionism*. Published by the Institute for Zionist Research, Tel Aviv, Autumn 1982. p. 179.

Chapter VIII

Solomon Schechter by Norman de Mattos Bentwich. Published by Allen & Unwin, Ltd., London, 1931. pp. 97, 104, 312.

Past and Present by Israel Friedlaender. Published by Ark Publishing Co., Cincinnati, 1919. p. 450.

Mordecai M. Kaplan: An Evaluation by Ira Eisenstein. Published by the Jewish Reconstructionist Foundation, New York, 1952. p. 298.

A Believing Jew by Milton Steinberg. Published by Harcourt, Brace, New York, 1951.

TABLE OF CONTENTS

EDITOR'S PREFACE

On the occasion of the fortieth anniversary of Israel's independence, the Youth Department felt it would be only natural to devote this year's sourcebook to Israel. We decided to concentrate on the age-old connection between the Jews and the land of Israel and focus on the various ways that connection has been made. We also wanted to describe how we, as Conservative Jews, express our attachment to *Eretz Yisrael* (the land of Israel).

I would like to thank the following people who read the manuscript and provided valuable comments.

Hezki Arieli
Rabbi Jerome M. Epstein
Rabbi Paul Freedman
Jules A. Gutin
Phil Jakar
David Keren
Rabbi Benjamin Z. Kreitman
Martin Kunoff
Rabbi Albert Lewis
Mirjam Mundstzuk-Orbach
Rabbi Joel Roth
Dr. Pesach Schindler
Rabbi Gerald Skolnik

I would like to take this opprtunity to thank Jules Gutin and Rabbi Paul Freedman who provided invaluable assistance in the final stages of the editing process. Marty Kunoff and Judith Sucher helped immeasurably with all the technical aspects of this book. Finally, my wife Lenore was always there when I needed her.

Jonah Layman

INTRODUCTION

Forty years! Already! I vividly recall that fifth of Iyyar (May 15) of 1948. Those of us who loved Zion and were part of one or another Zionist organization could not believe that a Jewish state was actually coming into being in our very own lifetime! Why, my grandfather and his before him, as well as his before him going all the way back to the first century, have prayed for this three times every day. Now, it was becoming a reality! What a *Zekhut* (privilege)! Indeed, at my ordination exercise at the Seminary shortly afterwards, "Hatikvah" was played for the first time at the graduation ceremony of the Jewish Theological Seminary.

How come? Why did the United States and the Soviet Union and other members of the United Nations permit the birth of the State of Israel? No one knows for sure. Some suggest that the Western nations had such guilt over the Holocaust that they felt the need to recompense the Jewish people. Others say that the Holocaust made the world keenly aware of the problems of Jewish homelessness. The nations therefore concluded that the Jews deserved one place they could call their own. They voted to divide Palestine into a small Jewish state and a large Arab state. Whatever their reasons, they were not the same as those that motivated world Jewry to fight for a homeland. These reasons came from deeper sources, from sources at the very heart of Judaism, from the dreams and prayers of the Jewish people for nearly two thousand years. The Jews may not have done very much to make those dreams and prayers come true. They waited for God to do that. They believed that the Messiah would come and miraculously transport them to Zion. They felt that it would be *hutzpah* for human beings to push God into action. But that passivity faded away to a large extent towards the end of the nineteenth century. In 1897, the World Zionist Organization was created and activities were undertaken to translate yearnings into reality. Jews began coming to *Eretz Yisrael* in larger numbers, to build the land physically, to engage in international diplomacy to create a state, to revive their language and culture.

The passionate attachment to Zion and the binding relationship of the people of Israel to the Land of Israel go back to the very beginnings of the Jewish people. The land was an intrinsic part of the covenant between God and Abraham and then between God and Abraham's children. There is a *midrash*, though taught centuries after the Patriarchs, which expresses the faith of Jews of all ages. It tells that Rabbi Shimon bar Yohai commented on a verse in Habakuk (3:6):

"He (i.e. God) rose and measured (or considered) the earth". The Holy One blessed be he considered all generations and found no people as fit to receive the Torah other than the people of Israel; the Holy One blessed be He, considered all generations and found no generation fit to receive the Torah as the generation of the wilderness; similarly, he

ר' שִׁמְעוֹן בֶּן יוֹחַי פָּתַח:
(חבקוק ג, ו) 'עָמַד וַיְמֹדֶד
אֶרֶץ רָאָה וַיַּתֵּר גּוֹיִם' —
מָדַד הַקָּדוֹשׁ בָּרוּךְ הוּא כָּל
הָאֻמּוֹת וְלֹא מָצָא אֻמָּה
שֶׁהָיְתָה רְאוּיָה לְקַבֵּל אֶת
הַתּוֹרָה אֶלָּא דּוֹר הַמִּדְבָּר;
מָדַד הַקָּדוֹשׁ בָּרוּךְ הוּא כָּל
הֶהָרִים וְלֹא מָצָא הַר שֶׁתִּנָּתֵן
בּוֹ אֶת הַתּוֹרָה אֶלָּא סִינַי;
מָדַד הַקָּדוֹשׁ בָּרוּךְ הוּא אֶת

11

considered all mountains and found none fit for His presence to dwell on other than the Temple mount; the Holy One blessed be He considered all cities and found none worthier of the Temple than Jerusalem... the Holy One blessed be he considered all lands, and found no land suitable to be given to Israel other than the land of Israel (*Vayikra Rabbah* 13:2)."

כָּל הֶעָיָרוֹת וְלֹא מָצָא עִיר שֶׁיִּבָּנֶה בּוֹ בֵּית הַמִּקְדָּשׁ אֶלָּא יְרוּשָׁלַיִם; מָדַד הַקָּדוֹשׁ בָּרוּךְ הוּא כָּל הָאֲרָצוֹת וְלֹא מָצָא אֶרֶץ שֶׁרְאוּיָה לִנָּתֵן לְיִשְׂרָאֵל אֶלָּא אֶרֶץ יִשְׂרָאֵל:

We are going to traverse all of Jewish history, period by period, and take note of those sources which reflect the Jewish perception of their universe: God, Torah, Israel and *Eretz Yisrael* inextricably bound together. As the famous biblical commentator Rashi (Rabbi Shlomo Yitzchaki, 1035-1104) put forth in his opening commentary to Genesis:

Rabbi Isaac said: The Torah should have opened with the verse 'This month shall be unto you the first of the months' (Ex.12:1), which is the first commandment given to Israel. What is the reason, then that it commences with the account of Creation? Because: 'He declared to His people the strength of His

אָמַר רַבִּי יִצְחָק: לֹא הָיָה צָרִיךְ לְהַתְחִיל אֶת הַתּוֹרָה אֶלָּא מֵהַחֹדֶשׁ הַזֶּה לָכֶם, שֶׁהִיא מִצְוָה רִאשׁוֹנָה שֶׁנִּצְטַווּ בָּהּ יִשְׂרָאֵל, וּמַה טַעַם פָּתַח בִּבְרֵאשִׁית? מִשּׁוּם כֹּחַ מַעֲשָׂיו הִגִּיד לְעַמּוֹ לָתֵת לָהֶם נַחֲלַת גּוֹיִם,

works in order that He might give them the heritage of the nations.' (Psalms 111:6) For should the peoples of the world say to Israel, 'You are robbers, because you took by force the lands of the nations of Canaan', Israel may reply to them: 'All the earth belongs to the Holy One blessed be He; He created it and gave it to whom He pleased. When He willed, He gave it to us.'

(תְּהִלִּים קי"א): שֶׁאָם יֹאמְרוּ אֻמּוֹת הָעוֹלָם לְיִשְׂרָאֵל: — לִסְטִים אַתֶּם, שֶׁכְּבַשְׁתֶּם אַרְצוֹת שִׁבְעָה גוֹיִם, הֵם אוֹמְרִים לָהֶם: — כָּל הָאָרֶץ שֶׁל הַקָּבָּ"ה הִיא, הוּא בְרָאָהּ. וּנְתָנָהּ לַאֲשֶׁר יָשַׁר בְּעֵינָיו, בִּרְצוֹנוֹ נְתָנָהּ לָהֶם וּבִרְצוֹנוֹ נְטָלָהּ מֵהֶם וּנְתָנָהּ לָנוּ:

13

THE BIBLE

Before examining the various books of the Bible, let us note that there is no word for Bible in Hebrew. That collection of sacred books is simply called "TANAKH" תנ"ך. Tanakh is not an actual word. Rather it is an acronym, made up of the first letter of the three sections that constitute the Bible. The first is TORAH (hence, the "ת"). It is followed by NEVIIM (Prophets), the "נ" being attached to the "T". The third section is called KETUVIM (Writings), the first letter of which is כ or ך. The three first letters are read as "Tanakh."

TORAH

Adam and Eve were given the opportunity of living an idyllic life in the Garden of Eden, but they chose to disobey the rules and were expelled. Their descendants had the ability to choose a Godly way, but they became so perverse that, with the exception of Noah and his family, they were destroyed by a flood. It was not long afterwards that God decided to select one particular people to live by His laws and thereby show others what loyalty to God truly meant.

The father of that people was Abraham, who, at the very beginning of his mission, was commanded to go to a new land where he would live according to his new insights.

Go forth from your native land and from your father's house to the land that I will show you. I will make of you a great nation and I will bless you.

(Gen. 12: 1-2)

וַיֹּאמֶר יהוה אֶל־אַבְרָם
לֶךְ־לְךָ   מֵאַרְצְךָ
וּמִמּוֹלַדְתְּךָ   וּמִבֵּית
אָבִיךָ אֶל־הָאָרֶץ אֲשֶׁר
אַרְאֶךָּ: וְאֶעֶשְׂךָ לְגוֹי
גָּדוֹל וַאֲבָרֶכְךָ

Abraham (then "Abram": his name was changed later) went with his wife, nephew and household. Life was not easy in the new surroundings. Enough is known today to recognize that the material progress of the Mesopotamia in which Abraham grew up was on a far higher level than that of Canaan, a relatively undeveloped area. Yet Canaan allowed for spiritual insights unattainable elsewhere. In Canaan, Abraham repeatedly heard God's voice and was repeatedly promised the Land.

I give all the land that you see to you and your offspring forever.......Up, walk about the land, through its length and its breadth, for I give it to you.

(Gen. 13: 15, 17)

כִּי אֶת־כָּל־הָאָרֶץ אֲשֶׁר־
אַתָּה רֹאֶה לְךָ אֶתְּנֶנָּה
וּלְזַרְעֲךָ עַד־עוֹלָם: קוּם
הִתְהַלֵּךְ בָּאָרֶץ לְאָרְכָּהּ
וּלְרָחְבָּהּ כִּי לְךָ אֶתְּנֶנָּה:

It was not enough for Abraham merely to feel

that he was entrusted with a divine mission. There had to be an expression of his relationship with God, something truly binding. That "something" was a *brit*, a covenant, a sacred accord between God and his chosen one. The covenant was reenforced more than once, and, whenever it was made, it included both Abraham's descendants and the Land.

I will maintain My covenant between Me and you, and your offspring to come, as an everlasting covenant throughout the ages, to be God to you and to your offspring to come. I assign the land you sojourn in to you and your offspring to come, all the land of Canaan, as an ever-lasting holding. I will be their God.

(Gen. 17:7-8)

וַהֲקִמֹתִי אֶת־בְּרִיתִי בֵּינִי וּבֵינֶךָ וּבֵין זַרְעֲךָ אַחֲרֶיךָ לְדֹרֹתָם לִבְרִית עוֹלָם לִהְיוֹת לְךָ לֵאלֹהִים וּלְזַרְעֲךָ אַחֲרֶיךָ וְנָתַתִּי לְךָ וּלְזַרְעֲךָ אַחֲרֶיךָ אֵת אֶרֶץ מְגֻרֶיךָ אֵת כָּל־ אֶרֶץ כְּנַעַן לַאֲחֻזַּת עוֹלָם וְהָיִיתִי לָהֶם לֵאלֹהִים:

When Sarah died, Abraham bought for her and for him their own burial sites; the Cave of Machpelah (facing Hebron). That purchase was the beginning of acquiring legal titles in the Land. When he had to find a wife for Isaac, he sent his trusted servant back to his family to find a suitable bride, but made it clear that Isaac was on no account to leave Canaan. Then, when Abraham died, he too was buried in the Cave of Machpelah as were his son Isaac and daughter-in-law Rebecca and their son Jacob and daughter-in-law Leah.

Jacob was also bound to the Land. He went

abroad and prospered but could not remain there simply because the economic situation was no good. He felt compelled to return. He and his family were destined for their own land. And, when he came back, God told him at Bethel:

The land that I assigned to Abraham and Isaac I assign to you; and to your offspring to come will I assign the land.
(Gen. 35:12)

וְאֶת־הָאָרֶץ אֲשֶׁר נָתַתִּי לְאַבְרָהָם וּלְיִצְחָק לְךָ אֶתְּנֶנָּה וּלְזַרְעֲךָ אַחֲרֶיךָ אֶתֵּן אֶת־הָאָרֶץ:

The children of Jacob (who God also called "Israel") were forced to move to Egypt temporarily when a famine at home became intense but they never expected to remain there. When Jacob died they took his body back to bury it in the Cave of Machpelah, and when Joseph died they preserved his body so they could take it for burial in their own land when they all went back. However, the Israelites were enslaved in Egypt. They continued to hope for return when Moses was commissioned by God to be the Liberator. He understood well what God was telling him:

I will bring you into the Land which I swore to give to Abraham, Isaac, and Jacob, and I will give it to you for a possession, I am the Lord.
(Exodus 6:8)

וְהֵבֵאתִי אֶתְכֶם אֶל־הָאָרֶץ אֲשֶׁר נָשָׂאתִי אֶת־יָדִי לָתֵת אֹתָהּ לְאַבְרָהָם לְיִצְחָק וּלְיַעֲקֹב וְנָתַתִּי אֹתָהּ לָכֶם מוֹרָשָׁה אֲנִי יהוה:

It was indeed difficult, but Moses succeeded in leading his people out of Egyptian slavery and in making of them a religious nation as they made their way to the Promised Land. They experienced Sinai and initiated a way of worshipping. They were commanded to follow many laws that encompassed the entirety life. But some of the rules were difficult to follow. Accepting a discipline, even though it be a sacred discipline, was at times too onerous for individuals or for the entire society. Therefore, The Torah frequently warned of the dangers of disobedience just as it promised rewards for hearkening to the laws of the Lord. Punishment meant exile, being scattered among various lands.

| You shall faithfully observe My laws and all my regulations, lest the land to which I bring you to settle in spew you out.
(Leviticus 20:22) | וּשְׁמַרְתֶּם אֶת־כָּל־חֻקֹּתַי וְאֶת־כָּל־מִשְׁפָּטַי וַעֲשִׂיתֶם אֹתָם וְלֹא־תָקִיא אֶתְכֶם הָאָרֶץ אֲשֶׁר אֲנִי מֵבִיא אֶתְכֶם שָׁמָּה לָשֶׁבֶת בָּהּ: |

In Deuteronomy, Moses is pictured as summarizing all of his teachings and the experiences of the people up until their crossing the Jordan. He finds it necessary to remind them again and again of how they are to behave when they settle and he reassures them about the qualities of the land they are inheriting.

| For the Lord your God is bringing you into a good land, a land with streams and springs and fountains issuing | כִּי יְהֹוָה אֱלֹהֶיךָ מְבִיאֲךָ אֶל־אֶרֶץ טוֹבָה אֶרֶץ נַחֲלֵי מָיִם עֲיָנֹת |

from plain and hill; a land of
wheat and barley, of vines,
figs and pomegranates, a land
of olive trees and honey; a
land where you may eat food
without stint, where you will
lack nothing, a land whose
rocks are iron and from whose
hills you can mine copper.
When you have eaten your
fill, give thanks to the Lord
your God for the good land
He has given you.

(Deut. 8:7-10)

וּתְהֹמֹת יֹצְאִים בַּבִּקְעָה
וּבָהָר: אֶרֶץ חִטָּה
וּשְׂעֹרָה וְגֶפֶן וּתְאֵנָה
וְרִמּוֹן אֶרֶץ־זֵית שֶׁמֶן
וּדְבָשׁ: אֶרֶץ אֲשֶׁר לֹא
בְמִסְכֵּנֻת תֹאכַל־בָּהּ
לֶחֶם לֹא־תֶחְסַר כֹּל בָּהּ
אֶרֶץ אֲשֶׁר אֲבָנֶיהָ בַרְזֶל
וּמֵהֲרָרֶיהָ תַּחְצֹב
נְחֹשֶׁת: וְאָכַלְתָּ וְשָׂבָעְתָּ
וּבֵרַכְתָּ אֶת־יהוה
אֱלֹהֶיךָ עַל־הָאָרֶץ
הַטֹּבָה אֲשֶׁר נָתַן־לָךְ:

B. PROPHETS

Moses was permitted to view the Land from the
top of Mt. Nebo (which is in the country called
Jordan today), but not to enter it. Instead, his
associate and successor, Joshua, led the Israelites
across the Jordan. Before proceeding with the task
following Moses' death, God communicated with him
and told him:

Be strong and resolute, for
you shall apportion to this
people the land that I swore to
their fathers to assign to them.

(Joshua 1:6)

חֲזַק וֶאֱמָץ כִּי אַתָּה
תַּנְחִיל אֶת־הָעָם הַזֶּה
אֶת־הָאָרֶץ אֲשֶׁר
נִשְׁבַּעְתִּי לַאֲבוֹתָם לָתֵת
לָהֶם:

Joshua was indeed strong and resolute and he

19

assigned to the tribes the sections of the land on which they settled. The Book of Joshua tells of the struggle of the Israelites to acquire their inheritance; the Books of Judges and Samuel relate how they lived before there was a kingdom; the Books of Kings give an account not only of David's establishing Jerusalem as the capital and Solomon's building the First Temple, but also of what took place until the fall of the Northern Kingdom (Israel) in 720 B.C.E. and the fall of the Southern Kingdom (Judea) in 586 B.C.E. During the latter part of this period, the remarkable messengers of God known as "prophets" preached their divine messages. They all demanded that the people of the Lord obey not only the letter of the Law but its spirit as well, that justice and mercy must pervade their lives as well as formal religious acts. Moreover, they insisted that injustice and immorality would result in destruction and exile. Nevertheless, that punishment would not be permanent; the time would come when Israel would be returned to its land and a better life would come into being.

In that day,	בַּיּוֹם הַהוּא אָקִים אֶת־
I will set up again the fallen booth of David:	סֻכַּת דָּוִיד הַנֹּפֶלֶת
I will mend its breaches and set up its ruins anew.	וְגָדַרְתִּי אֶת־פִּרְצֵיהֶן וַהֲרִסֹתָיו אָקִים
I will build it firm as in the days of old. ...	וּבְנִיתִיהָ כִּימֵי עוֹלָם׃
I will restore My people Israel.	וְשַׁבְתִּי אֶת־שְׁבוּת עַמִּי
They shall rebuild ruined cities and inhabit them;	יִשְׂרָאֵל וּבָנוּ עָרִים נְשַׁמּוֹת וְיָשָׁבוּ וְנָטְעוּ
They shall plant vineyards and drink their wine;	כְרָמִים וְשָׁתוּ אֶת־יֵינָם וְעָשׂוּ גַנּוֹת וְאָכְלוּ אֶת־

They shall till gardens and eat their fruits,
And I will plant them upon their soil,
Nevermore to be uprooted
From the soil I have give them
Said the Lord your God.

(Amos 9:11, 14-15)

פְּרִיהֶם: וּנְטַעְתִּים עַל־
אַדְמָתָם וְלֹא יִנָּתְשׁוּ
עוֹד מֵעַל אַדְמָתָם אֲשֶׁר
נָתַתִּי לָהֶם אָמַר יהוה
אֱלֹהֶיךָ:

Isaiah lived not long after Amos in the eighth pre-Christian century. It is evident that he was a cultured Jerusalemite who united a profound knowledge of the world with profound religious feelings. With great passion and genius, he strove to lead his people in the ways of God and to impose the Divine will upon the conduct of the State. When he pictured a glorious future, it was one centered in Zion:

In the days to come, The Mount of the Lord's House Shall stand firm above the mountains. And tower above the hills And all the nations Shall gaze upon it with joy. And the many peoples shall go and shall say: "Come, Let us go up to the Mount of the Lord, To the House of the God of Jacob; That He may instruct us in His ways, And that we may walk in His paths." For instruc-

וְהָיָה בְּאַחֲרִית הַיָּמִים נָכוֹן
יִהְיֶה הַר בֵּית־יהוה בְּרֹאשׁ
הֶהָרִים וְנִשָּׂא מִגְּבָעוֹת וְנָהֲרוּ
אֵלָיו כָּל־הַגּוֹיִם: וְהָלְכוּ עַמִּים
רַבִּים וְאָמְרוּ לְכוּ וְנַעֲלֶה אֶל־
הַר־יהוה אֶל־בֵּית אֱלֹהֵי
יַעֲקֹב וְיוֹרֵנוּ מִדְּרָכָיו וְנֵלְכָה
בְּאֹרְחֹתָיו כִּי מִצִּיּוֹן תֵּצֵא
תוֹרָה וּדְבַר־יהוה מִירוּשָׁלָיִם:

tion shall come forth
from Zion, The word of
the Lord from Jerusalem.

(Isaiah 2:2-3)

Foreseeing the day when the Children of Israel
would suffer in exile, Isaiah also foresaw the day
when they would come home.

And in that day, a great ram's
horn shall be sounded; and
the strayed who are in the
land of Assyria and the
expelled who are in the land of
Egypt shall come and worship
the Lord on the holy mount,
in Jerusalem.

(Isaiah 27:13)

וְהָיָה בַּיּוֹם הַהוּא יִתָּקַע
בְּשׁוֹפָר גָּדוֹל וּבָאוּ
הָאֹבְדִים בְּאֶרֶץ אַשּׁוּר
וְהַנִּדָּחִים בְּאֶרֶץ מִצְרָיִם
וְהִשְׁתַּחֲווּ לַיהוה בְּהַר
הַקֹּדֶשׁ בִּירוּשָׁלָיִם:

A little more than a century after Isaiah, another
prophet thundered messages of impending doom:
Jeremiah. He was the last prophet before the
destruction of the Temple and Jerusalem in 586 B.C.E.
and personally witnessed the horrible destruction he
himself had proclaimed. Still, he had confidence in the
future. True, people hated what Jeremiah said; he was
even charged with being a traitor. Nevertheless, he
maintained an unshakable faith that God would some
day restore Israel.

Though I have rejected you, I
will take you, One from a
town and two from a clan and
bring you to Zion. ...At that

שׁוּבוּ בָנִים שׁוֹבָבִים
נְאֻם-יהוה כִּי אָנֹכִי
בָּעַלְתִּי בָכֶם וְלָקַחְתִּי

time, they shall call Jerusalem "Throne of the Lord" and all nations shall assemble there, in the name of the Lord, at Jerusalem. They shall no longer follow the willfulness of their evil hearts. In those days, the House of Judah shall go with the House of Israel; they shall come together from the land of the north to the land I gave your fathers as a possession.

(Jeremiah 3:14, 17-18)

And I Myself will gather the remnant of My flock from all the lands to which I have banished them, and I shall bring them back to their pasture, where they shall be fertile and increase. ...See, a time is coming — declares the Lord — when I will raise up a true branch of David's line. He shall reign as king and shall prosper, and he shall do what is right and just in the land. In his days Judah shall be delivered and Israel shall dwell secure. And this is the name by which he shall be called: "The Lord is our Vindicator."

(Jeremiah 23:3, 5-6)

אֶתְכֶם אֶחָד מֵעִיר
וּשְׁנַיִם מִמִּשְׁפָּחָה
וְהֵבֵאתִי אֶתְכֶם צִיּוֹן:
בָּעֵת הַהִיא יִקְרְאוּ
לִירוּשָׁלַיִם כִּסֵּא יהוה
וְנִקְווּ אֵלֶיהָ כָל־הַגּוֹיִם
לְשֵׁם יהוה לִירוּשָׁלָיִם
וְלֹא־יֵלְכוּ עוֹד אַחֲרֵי
שְׁרִרוּת לִבָּם הָרָע:
בַּיָּמִים הָהֵמָּה יֵלְכוּ
בֵית־יְהוּדָה עַל־בֵּית
יִשְׂרָאֵל וְיָבֹאוּ יַחְדָּו
מֵאֶרֶץ צָפוֹן עַל־הָאָרֶץ
אֲשֶׁר הִנְחַלְתִּי אֶת־
אֲבוֹתֵיכֶם:

וַאֲנִי אֲקַבֵּץ אֶת־שְׁאֵרִית
צֹאנִי מִכֹּל הָאֲרָצוֹת
אֲשֶׁר־הִדַּחְתִּי אֹתָם שָׁם
וַהֲשִׁבֹתִי אֶתְהֶן עַל־נְוֵהֶן
וּפָרוּ וְרָבוּ:
הִנֵּה יָמִים בָּאִים נְאֻם
יהוה וַהֲקִמֹתִי לְדָוִד
צֶמַח צַדִּיק וּמָלַךְ מֶלֶךְ
וְהִשְׂכִּיל וְעָשָׂה מִשְׁפָּט
וּצְדָקָה בָּאָרֶץ: בְּיָמָיו
תִּוָּשַׁע יְהוּדָה וְיִשְׂרָאֵל
יִשְׁכֹּן לָבֶטַח וְזֶה־שְּׁמוֹ
אֲשֶׁר־יִקְרְאוֹ יהוה
צִדְקֵנוּ:

23

The First Temple was destroyed in 586 B.C.E. by the great Babylonian Empire. But its ruler, Nebuchadnezzar, had invaded the country and conquered Jerusalem once before, a decade earlier. At that time, in 597 B.C.E., he took the king of Judah and many of the capital's most prominent people into exile. Among them was a *kohen* (priest) named Ezekiel, a man of extraordinary spiritual insights and gifted communicative abilities. As a prophet, one commissioned to be God's messenger, Ezekiel, when a young man, prophesied the destruction of Jerusalem due to the sins of the people. After calamity struck, the more mature prophet foresaw the resurrection of the nation and its glorious future. But even when he was proclaiming doom he brought a note of hope.

Thus said the Lord God: I will gather you from the peoples and assemble you out of the countries where you havebeen scattered, and I will give you the Land of Israel.

לָכֵן אֱמֹר כֹּה־אָמַר אֲדֹנָי יְהוִֹה וְקִבַּצְתִּי אֶתְכֶם מִן־הָעַמִּים וְאָסַפְתִּי אֶתְכֶם מִן־הָאֲרָצוֹת אֲשֶׁר נְפֹצוֹתֶם בָּהֶם וְנָתַתִּי לָכֶם אֶת־אַדְמַת יִשְׂרָאֵל:

(Ezekiel 11:17)

Ezekiel was a mystic. His visions were sometimes clouded but at other times very clear, as when he described in detail the future Temple that would arise. One of the most familiar of Ezekiel's prophecies is the vision of the valley of the dry bones. The prophet tells of being carried into a valley full of bones and hearing God ask him: "Can these bones live?" He does not know how to answer but the divine voice tells him that they will be covered with sinews and flesh and spirit. He sees this done and understands that the image of resurrection is that of the people of Israel being redeemed and restored.

Prophesy, therefore, and say to them: Thus said the Lord God: I am going to open your graves and lift you out of the graves, O My people, and bring you to the Land of Israel. ...I will put My breath in you and you shall live again and I will set you upon your own soil. ... Thus said the Lord God: I am going to take the Israelite people from among the nations they have gone to and gather them from every quarter, and bring them to their own land. ... Then they shall be My people and I will be their God.

(Ezekiel 37:12, 14, 21, 23)

לָכֵן הִנָּבֵא וְאָמַרְתָּ אֲלֵיהֶם
כֹּה־אָמַר אֲדֹנָי יהוה הִנֵּה
אֲנִי פֹתֵחַ אֶת־קִבְרוֹתֵיכֶם
וְהַעֲלֵיתִי אֶתְכֶם מִקִּבְרוֹתֵיכֶם
עַמִּי וְהֵבֵאתִי אֶתְכֶם אֶל־
אַדְמַת יִשְׂרָאֵל:
וְנָתַתִּי רוּחִי בָכֶם וִחְיִיתֶם
וְהִנַּחְתִּי אֶתְכֶם עַל־אַדְמַתְכֶם
וִידַעְתֶּם כִּי אֲנִי יהוה דִּבַּרְתִּי
וְעָשִׂיתִי נְאֻם־יהוה:
וְדַבֵּר אֲלֵיהֶם כֹּה־אָמַר אֲדֹנָי
יהוה הִנֵּה אֲנִי לֹקֵחַ אֶת־
בְּנֵי יִשְׂרָאֵל מִבֵּין הַגּוֹיִם
אֲשֶׁר הָלְכוּ־שָׁם וְקִבַּצְתִּי
אֹתָם מִסָּבִיב וְהֵבֵאתִי אוֹתָם
אֶל־אַדְמָתָם:
וְלֹא יִטַּמְּאוּ עוֹד בְּגִלּוּלֵיהֶם
וּבְשִׁקּוּצֵיהֶם וּבְכֹל פִּשְׁעֵיהֶם
וְהוֹשַׁעְתִּי אֹתָם מִכֹּל
מוֹשְׁבֹתֵיהֶם אֲשֶׁר חָטְאוּ בָהֶם
וְטִהַרְתִּי אוֹתָם וְהָיוּ־לִי לְעָם
וַאֲנִי אֶהְיֶה לָהֶם לֵאלֹהִים:

Within five decades following the Fall of Jerusalem, Babylonia was defeated by the Persians whose king, Cyrus, allowed those Jews who so wished to return to Judea. Many were full of joy and envisioned a wonderful new Zion coming into being. Among them was the eloquent prophet, Isaiah II, who announced that Jerusalem has grieved enough and is ready for consolation. (Some scholars claim that the content and context from chapter 40 of Isaiah and following reflect a different period of time than the first 39 chapters, and that, therefore, the Isaiah of chapter 40 ff. must be a different Isaiah, Isaiah II.)

Ascend a lofty mountain, O herald of joy to Zion; Raise your voice with power, O herald of joy to Jerusalem — Raise it, have no fear; Announce to the cities of Judah: Behold your God!

עַל הַר־גָּבֹהַּ עֲלִי־לָךְ מְבַשֶּׂרֶת צִיּוֹן הָרִימִי בַכֹּחַ קוֹלֵךְ מְבַשֶּׂרֶת יְרוּשָׁלַיִם הָרִימִי אַל־ תִּירָאִי אִמְרִי לְעָרֵי יְהוּדָה הִנֵּה אֱלֹהֵיכֶם:

(Isaiah 40:9)

C. PSALMS

The Book of Psalms is a lyrical anthology containing the outpouring of Jewish hearts seeking to share with God a host of concerns, both individual and collective. Traditionally, the authorship of the entire book of Psalms (150 chapters) is ascribed to David, but biblical scholars claim that due to the content and style of many of the psalms, David could not have written them. The various poets sing of joy and grief, confidence and fear, hope and despair. They touch on matters that are personal and those that express love of Zion. Abba Eban, the noted Israeli statesman, once noted that they achieved "the unparalleled gift of expressing the intimately Hebraic spirit of the people known to history as 'peculiar', and, at one and the same time, playing on the heartstrings of mankind entire. In this Book, the national and the universal dwell side by side, inseparable and neither contradicting the other."

The psalms that are most joyous and most confident are those that sing of Jerusalem and Zion.

I rejoiced when they said to me,
"We are going to the House of the Lord."
Our feet stood inside your gates, O Jerusalem, Jerusalem built up, a city knit together, To which tribes would make pilgrimage, the tribes of the Lord, — as was enjoined upon Israel — to praise the name of the Lord. There the thrones of judgement stood, thrones of the house of David. Pray for the well-being of Jerusalem; "May those who love you be at peace. May there be well-being within your ramparts, peace in your citadels. For the sake of my kin and my friends, I pray for your well-being; for the sake of the house of the Lord our God, I seek your good.

(Psalm 122)

שִׁיר הַמַּעֲלוֹת לְדָוִד
שָׂמַחְתִּי בְּאֹמְרִים לִי
בֵּית יהוה נֵלֵךְ: עֹמְדוֹת
הָיוּ רַגְלֵינוּ בִּשְׁעָרַיִךְ
יְרוּשָׁלָיִם: יְרוּשָׁלַיִם
הַבְּנוּיָה כְּעִיר שֶׁחֻבְּרָה־
לָּהּ יַחְדָּו: שֶׁשָּׁם עָלוּ
שְׁבָטִים שִׁבְטֵי־יָהּ עֵדוּת
לְיִשְׂרָאֵל לְהֹדוֹת לְשֵׁם
יהוה: כִּי שָׁמָּה יָשְׁבוּ
כִסְאוֹת לְמִשְׁפָּט כִּסְאוֹת
לְבֵית דָּוִד: שַׁאֲלוּ שְׁלוֹם
יְרוּשָׁלָיִם יִשְׁלָיוּ אֹהֲבָיִךְ:
יְהִי־שָׁלוֹם בְּחֵילֵךְ שַׁלְוָה
בְּאַרְמְנוֹתָיִךְ: לְמַעַן אַחַי
וְרֵעָי אֲדַבְּרָה־נָּא שָׁלוֹם
בָּךְ: לְמַעַן בֵּית־יהוה
אֱלֹהֵינוּ אֲבַקְשָׁה טוֹב
לָךְ:

Other ancient peoples were defeated and thereupon became assimilated into the society of the stronger power. Not so the Israelites. Even in exile they preserved their identity and maintained their faith in the God of Israel. Even in exile they yearned for Zion and prayed to return to it.

By the rivers of Babylon, there we sat, sat and wept, as we thought of Zion. There on the poplars we hung up our lyres, for our captors asked us there for songs, our tormentors, for amusement, "Sing us one of the songs of Zion" How can we sing a song of the Lord on alien soil?
If I forget you, O Jerusalem, let my right hand wither; let my tongue stick to my palate if I cease to think of you, if I do not keep Jerusalem in memory even at my happiest hour.

(Psalm 137: 1-6)

עַל־נַהֲרוֹת בָּבֶל שָׁם יָשַׁבְנוּ גַּם־בָּכִינוּ בְּזָכְרֵנוּ אֶת־צִיּוֹן: עַל־עֲרָבִים בְּתוֹכָהּ תָּלִינוּ כִּנֹּרוֹתֵינוּ: כִּי שָׁם שְׁאֵלוּנוּ שׁוֹבֵינוּ דִּבְרֵי־ שִׁיר וְתוֹלָלֵינוּ שִׂמְחָה שִׁירוּ לָנוּ מִשִּׁיר צִיּוֹן: אֵיךְ נָשִׁיר אֶת־שִׁיר־ יהוה עַל אַדְמַת נֵכָר: אִם־אֶשְׁכָּחֵךְ יְרוּשָׁלַיִם תִּשְׁכַּח יְמִינִי: תִּדְבַּק לְשׁוֹנִי לְחִכִּי אִם־לֹא אֶזְכְּרֵכִי אִם־לֹא אַעֲלֶה אֶת־יְרוּשָׁלַיִם עַל רֹאשׁ שִׂמְחָתִי:

Discussion Questions

1) If the prophets loved their people so dearly, why were they such sharp critics? Can we love Israel deeply but disagree with some of the actions the government undertakes? Should we keep our disagreements to ourselves and only agree with Israel in public?

2) What do we learn from the Patriarchs' desire to be buried in Israel? Why are there people today

who still desire to be buried in Israel? (see Rabbinic sources in chapter II)

3) How significant is it today to claim that we were promised the land of Israel in the Bible? Does that statement weaken or strengthen our claim to the land?

4) What do you think the significance is of these verses appearing in the liturgy? How do you feel when you recite them? Do you agree or disagree with the sentiments expressed?

5) Many Christians accept the Hebrew Bible (which they call the "Old Testament") as sacred. If so, what do you think their commitment to Israel should be? After reading these sources from the Tanakh, do you think it is possible for a believing Christian to be anti-Zionist?

RABBINIC PERIOD

The Jewish tradition has always regarded the books of the Bible as sacred. Why? Did our ancestors actually hear its words trumpeted from the heavens or did God deliver His messages through a human messenger? Perhaps no one can ever prove the answers to such questions, but traditionally, Jews have always believed that the commandments, teachings and ethics of the Bible were divine and therefore binding. But that did not mean that everything was simple and clear. For example, it was forbidden to work on the Sabbath but what exactly was considered "work"? The Torah permitted marriage and divorce but it did not state what the precise procedures were. It implied what we know as *talit* and *tefillin* but it gave no specifications for them.

There were many laws couched in language that was abstract or generalized, the application of which required further details. Moreover, there were instructions that required adaptation or adjustment with the change of times and confrontation with new cultures within the framework of *halacha* (Jewish law). Living independently was not the same as living under the Persians or the Greeks. The attraction of

Hellenism presented new challenges to Jews committed to God and to Torah. At all times, the Jewish tradition had to reckon with other cultures and civilizations.

When people wanted to know what to do and how to act, when they had questions and wanted to clarify understanding of verses, they turned to their teachers and leaders. In every generation, authoritative men arose to answer questions, to decide matters of law, to interpret and comment on Scriptures. By the first century of the Common Era, if not before, these men were called "rabbis" (rav means "master" and rabee means "my teacher"). Each gained his title by studying with a previous authority who decided when his disciple deserved ordination. Each taught, explained and decided matters of law.

Although rabbis continued to be ordained throughout the centuries, the first five hundred years of the Common Era is called "the Rabbinic Period". That is because those were the years in which the Talmud came into being. Actually, there are two Talmudim. The one produced in Eretz Yisrael (called Talmud Yerushalmi) was concluded about 400 C.E. The other, produced in Babylonia (and therefore called Talmud Bavli), received its final editing in 499 C.E.

They both accept the Mishnah, the arrangement of Jewish law undertaken by Rabbi Judah the Nasi (president, leader of the Sanhedrin) at the end of the second and beginning of the third century. In the schools of Eretz Yisrael and of Babylonia, scholars plumbed the depths of each mishnah and discussed at length its meaning and implications. These discussions plus anecdotes and legends together with ethical and theological observations were collected into a work known as Gemara. The Mishna and Gemara together constitute the *Talmud*.

The Talmudic discussions stem from cases cited in the Mishnah. At the same time, there was another kind of rabbinic discourse called Midrash. It stemmed from a verse in the Bible and was either a commentary or a sermon. Both the Midrash and the Talmud reflect rabbinic thought and rabbinic decisions in all matters of life. Rabbinic jurisprudence encompasses what is today often divided into sacred and secular but is regarded as a whole by the Jewish tradition. The Talmud and Midrash are the basis of all of Judaism ever since.

The rabbis dealt with matters of concern to each individual personally and to those affecting the Jewish people as a whole. They loved the Land of Israel with great passion for they were convinced that God had destined Israel for that land.

Our rabbis taught: One should always live in *Eretz Yisrael* even in a city where the majority are non-Jews and not live outside the Land even in a city where the majority are Jews. Whoever lives in *Eretz Yisrael* is as one who has God while whoever lives outside *Eretz Yisrael* is as one who does not have God.	תָּ"ר לְעוֹלָם יָדוּר אָדָם בְּא"י אֲפִי' בְּעִיר שֶׁרוּבָּהּ עוֹבְדֵי כּוֹכָבִים, וְאַל יָדוּר בְּחוּ"ל וְאֲפִילוּ בְּעִיר שֶׁרוּבָּהּ יִשְׂרָאֵל, שֶׁכָּל הַדָּר בְּאֶרֶץ יִשְׂרָאֵל דּוֹמֶה כְּמִי שֶׁיֵּשׁ לוֹ אֱלוֹהַּ, וְכָל הַדָּר בְּחוּצָה לָאָרֶץ דּוֹמֶה כְּמִי שֶׁאֵין לוֹ אֱלוֹהַּ.

(Talmud Bavli, Ketubot 110b)

It is better to spend the night   מוּטָב לָלוּן בַּמִּדְבָּרוֹת

in the wilderness of *Eretz Israel* than to spend the night in palaces outside *Eretz Yisrael.*

שֶׁל אֶרֶץ יִשְׂרָאֵל וְלֹא בְּפָלָטִיּוֹת שֶׁל חוּצָה לָאָרֶץ.

(Midrash Bereishit Rabbah 39)

The story is told of R. Yehuda ben Beteira and R. Matya ben Heresh and R. Hanina ben Ahi, R. Yehoshua and R. Yonatan. They were traveling from the Land, arrived at a place named Platus, and remembered *Eretz Yisrael.* They turned their eyes toward it and wept. They tore their garments and recited this verse: "You shall inherit and dwell therein, and you shall observe all the laws". They returned home and concluded: Dwelling in *Eretz Yisrael* outweighs all the commandments of the Torah.

מַעֲשֶׂה בְּרַ' יְהוּדָה בֶּן בְּתֵרָא וְרַ' מַתִּיָא בֶּן חֶרֶשׁ וְרַ' חֲנִינָא בֶּן אַחִי, רַ' יְהוֹשֻׁעַ וְרַ' יוֹנָתָן שֶׁהָיוּ יוֹצְאִים חוּצָה לָאָרֶץ וְהִגִּיעוּ לִפְלָטוּס וְזָכְרוּ אֶת אֶרֶץ יִשְׂרָאֵל, זָקְפוּ עֵינֵיהֶם וְזָלְגוּ דִמְעוֹתֵיהֶם וְקָרְעוּ בִּגְדֵיהֶם וְקָרְאוּ הַמִּקְרָא הַזֶּה: "וִירִשְׁתֶּם אֹתָהּ וִישַׁבְתֶּם בָּהּ, וּשְׁמַרְתֶּם לַעֲשׂוֹת אֶת כָּל הַחֻקִּים." וְחָזְרוּ וּבָאוּ לִמְקוֹמָם אָמְרוּ יְשִׁיבַת אֶרֶץ יִשְׂרָאֵל שְׁקוּלָה כְּנֶגֶד כָּל הַמִּצְוֹת שֶׁבַּתּוֹרָה. (ספרי ראה)

(Midrash Sifrei R'ay)

Prof. Gerson Cohen has observed: "The rabbis could no more conceive of Judaism without the *land* of Israel than they could have without the *people* of Israel." They were not able to imagine God arranging things in any other way.

The Holy One blessed be He said: A small group in *Eretz Yisrael* is dearer to me than a Great Sanhedrin outside the Land.

(Talmud Yerushalmi, Nedarim 6:8)

אָמַר הַקָּדוֹשׁ־בָּרוּךְ־הוּא: חֲבִיבָה עָלַי כַּת קְטַנָּה שֶׁבְּאֶרֶץ יִשְׂרָאֵל מִסַּנְהֶדְרִין גְּדוֹלָה שֶׁבְּחוּצָה לָאָרֶץ.

(ירוש׳ נדר׳ פ״ו, ה״ח)

We have learned, R. Eliezer the Great says: "Such is the story of heaven and earth when they were created — when the Lord God made earth and heaven." (Genesis 2:4) The story of the heaven is that it was created from the earth. But the sages say: Both were created out of Zion, as it says: "God, the Lord God spoke and summoned the world from east to west" (Psalms 50:1). They continue to quote: "From Zion, perfect in beauty, God appeared." (Psalms 50:2). Thus we learn that the beauty of the world is included in it.

(Talmud Bavli Yoma 54b)

תַּנְיָא, רַבִּי אֱלִיעֶזֶר הַגָּדוֹל אוֹמֵר: ״אֵלֶּה תוֹלְדוֹת הַשָּׁמַיִם וְהָאָרֶץ בְּהִבָּרְאָם בְּיוֹם עֲשׂוֹת ה׳ אֱלֹהִים אֶרֶץ וְשָׁמַיִם״. תּוֹלְדוֹת שָׁמַיִם — מִשָּׁמַיִם נִבְרְאוּ, תּוֹלְדוֹת הָאָרֶץ — מֵאֶרֶץ נִבְרָאוּ. וַחֲכָמִים אוֹמְרִים: אֵלּוּ וָאֵלּוּ מִצִּיּוֹן נִבְרְאוּ, שֶׁנֶּאֱמַר, ״מִזְמוֹר לְאָסָף אֵל אֱלֹהִים ה׳ דִּבֶּר וַיִּקְרָא אָרֶץ מִמִּזְרַח שֶׁמֶשׁ עַד מְבֹאוֹ״ וְאוֹמֵר ״מִצִּיּוֹן מִכְלַל יֹפִי אֱלֹהִים הוֹפִיעַ״ — מִמֶּנּוּ מוּכְלָל יוֹפְיוֹ שֶׁל עוֹלָם.

When the rabbis dreamt of the Messiah, they spoke of him appearing only in *Eretz Yisrael*. Those

who believed in the resurrection of the dead were
certain that the miracle would take place in the Land
of Israel and that the bones of those so unfortunate as
not to be buried there would have to roll through
underground passages to reach the point of
resurrection.

Our sages said in the name of
R. Helbo: Why did our fathers
so desire to be buried in *Eretz
Yisrael*? Because the dead
there will come to life first in
the days of the Messiah and
they will enjoy the Messiah.
R. Hanina said: Whoever dies
outside the Land and is buried
there suffers a double death.

(Midrash Bereishit Rabbah 96)

אָמְרוּ רַבּוֹתֵינוּ שְׁנֵי
דְּבָרִים בְּשֵׁם רַ' חֶלְבּוֹ:
לָמָּה הָאָבוֹת מְחַבְּבִין
קְבוּרַת אֶרֶץ יִשְׂרָאֵל,
שֶׁמֵּתֵי אֶרֶץ יִשְׂרָאֵל
חַיִּים תְּחִלָּה בִּימוֹת
הַמָּשִׁיחַ, וְאוֹכְלִין שְׁנוֹת
הַמָּשִׁיחַ; רַ' חֲנִינָא
אָמַר: מִי שֶׁמֵּת בְּחוּצָה
לָאָרֶץ וְנִקְבַּר שָׁם, שְׁתֵּי
מִיתוֹת יֵשׁ בְּיָדוֹ.

Rabbis often commented on the appropriateness
of the people and the Land. They regarded each as
made for the other.

The Holy One blessed be He
said to Moses: The Land is
dear to Me and Israel is dear
to Me. I will bring Israel
which is dear to Me into the
land which is dear to Me.

(Midrash Bamidbar Rabbah 23)

אָמַר לוֹ הַקָּדוֹשׁ בָּרוּךְ
הוּא לְמֹשֶׁה: הֵן הָאָרֶץ
חֲבִיבָה עָלַי, וְיִשְׂרָאֵל
חֲבִיבִין עָלַי, אֲנִי אַכְנִיס
אֶת יִשְׂרָאֵל, שֶׁהֵן
חֲבִיבִין עָלַי, לָאָרֶץ,
שֶׁחֲבִיבָה עָלַי.

R. Simlai expounded: Why did Moses so desire to enter *Eretz Yisrael?* Did he need its fruits or its bounty? No — this is what Moses said: There are many *Mitzvot* (commandments) that Israel has been commanded which can be fulfilled only in the Land. Permit me to enter that I too may fulfill them personally."

(Sotah 14a)

דָּרַשׁ רַבִּי שִׂמְלַאי מִפְּנֵי מַה נִתְאַוָּה מֹשֶׁה רַבֵּינוּ לִיכָּנֵס לְאָ"יִ? וְכִי לַאֲכוֹל מִפְּרִיָהּ הוּא צָרִיךְ אוֹ לִשְׂבּוֹעַ מִטוּבָהּ הוּא צָרִיךְ; אֶלָּא כָּךְ אָמַר מֹשֶׁה הַרְבֵּה מִצְוֹת נִצְטַוּוּ יִשְׂרָאֵל וְאֵין מִתְקַיְימִין אֶלָּא בְּאָ"יִ, אֶכָּנֵס אֲנִי לָאָרֶץ כְּדֵי שֶׁיִּתְקַיְימוּ כּוּלָן עַל יָדִי.

So important was living in *Eretz Yisrael* that Jewish law permitted what would otherwise have been prohibited in order to enable settlement. Although writing and conducting business was strictly forbidden on the Sabbath the rabbis held that, if one was acquiring a house in *Eretz Yisrael,* one could write out the bill of the sale on *Shabbat* (Talmud Bavli Baba Kamma 80b).

If a man living outside the Land wanted to make *aliyah* but his wife refused, she must either reconsider and go with him or receive a divorce and forfeit payment of her marriage contract. The same rule applied to a couple living in *Eretz Yisrael* if one of them wanted to leave: the law was behind the one remaining in the country. Migration was deemed a religious infraction.

Whether the Jews actually had freedom in their own land or had to live under rule of a conqueror, whether they were able to dwell in *Eretz Yisrael* or were forced into exile, they never surrendered their claim. They were convinced that God had chosen them for the Land of Israel.

The rabbis insisted that even studying, that *mitzvah* of prime importance, is enhanced when practiced in the Holy Land.

There is no Torah like the Torah of *Eretz Yisrael* and no wisdom like the wisdom of *Eretz Yisrael*.

(Sifrei Ekev)

אֵין תּוֹרָה כְּתוֹרַת אֶרֶץ יִשְׂרָאֵל וְאֵין חָכְמָה כְּחָכְמַת אֶרֶץ יִשְׂרָאֵל.

(ספרי עקב)

Ten measures of wisdom descended into the world — *Eretz Yisrael* took nine and one was left for the rest of the world"

(Talmud Bavli, Kiddushin 49b)

עֲשָׂרָה קַבִּים חָכְמָה יָרְדוּ לָעוֹלָם, תִּשְׁעָה נָטְלָה אֶרֶץ יִשְׂרָאֵל וְאֶחָד כָּל הָעוֹלָם כּוּלוֹ.

The attitude of the rabbis is reflected in a comment of one of the foremost religious leaders of the nineteenth century, Rabbi Shmuel Mohilever. He quoted a rabbinic interpretation of a phrase in the Torah. The Book of Genesis tells that Jacob, after serving Laban for many years in Aram, returned home and had to face his brother Esau. The text says: "And Jacob was sorely afraid" (Gen. 32:8). The rabbis wanted to explain why the righteous Jacob should have feared his brother and they thought of him saying: "Esau has lived in *Eretz Yisrael* all these years. Perhaps, by virtue of that, he will overcome me."

Rabbi Mohilever proceeded to point out that this

could be perplexing. Here was Jacob who observed all the commandments even while living with a scoundrel like Laban. Why should he have feared Esau who only kept one *mitzvah*, one commandment, that of living in *Eretz Yisrael?* Rabbi Mohilever thereupon concluded that this commandment, even if observed by an Esau, outweighs many others, even though a righteous man such as Jacob observed them.

In the year 70, Jerusalem was captured by Rome and the Temple was destroyed. That could have meant the end of the Jewish people and of Judaism. The beloved capital was captured. The center of religion, the sanctuary, disappeared. Many survivors lost their nearest and dearest or else saw them carted off to be sold as slaves or to amuse Roman crowds as prey for lions. It seemed as though the pagans had finally triumphed and the children of the covenant were completely vanquished. One might also expect them to have subsequently abandoned the God of Israel and to have made no further efforts to perpetuate their heritage.

However, this was not the case. To be sure, the survivors mourned. Not only did they mourn, but so did their children and their children's children and all their descendants down to the present day. The anniversary of the destruction of the Temple, Tisha B'Av, became the blackest day of the Jewish calendar, a day of fasting and reciting dirges. On other occasions as well the bitter day was vividly recalled. There were pious Jews who left unpainted a spot on the eastern wall of their homes as a symbol of mourning for the Temple and Jerusalem. The three weeks preceding Tisha B'Av were a period of annual mourning for the entire Jewish people, especially the concluding nine days.

Yet, despite the sorrow, the Jews did not view life pessimistically, nor did they surrender their faith in God. To the contrary, their love of Him, as well as their love of Torah and of Zion, became more intense. Palestine continued its focal role and, long after that terrible day in the summer of 70, its schools went on providing instruction and light for all.

The Roman victory did not lead to the expulsion of all Jews from Palestine. To the contrary, Jews continued to constitute the majority for three more centuries and remained an important minority afterward. The rabbis were their leaders and at their head was a dignitary with the title "Nasi" (Patriarch). The *Nasi* served as the official liaison with Rome; he was recognized by the ruling power as the representative and chief official of the Jewish people. The institution of the patriarchate was maintained for nearly four centuries, indicating Rome's continued recognition of Palestine as the center of Judaism and of the Jews.

One might ask: Once the Romans displayed their military might, did the Jews become utterly submissive? Did they reconcile themselves to their loss and dutifully obey their overlords? No doubt some did; they wanted to live as quietly as possible. But many did not. They refused to accept foreign domination passively and looked for ways to regain independence. They therefore planned revolts and from time to time rose up against the conqueror.

The year 115 seemed to be an auspicious moment to get rid of the Romans. Rome was having trouble in the Near East and a coalition of recently subdued peoples joined together to challenge Roman supremacy. Thinking Rome would be so absorbed with that threat that she would not be able to pay attention to Palestine, the Jews revolted. They had obtained the assistance of Jews in Egypt and Babylonia but they were still no match for the imperial forces and the revolt failed. Nevertheless, the Jews exacted such a heavy toll that Emperor Trajan's eastern campaign collapsed and his power was considerably weakened.

Just as the Roman victory 45 years earlier had not resulted in Jewish submission, so too the victory of 115 did not stifle the Jewish determination to regain their freedom in their own land. Secret plans were concocted and 17 years later, in 132, there was another revolt — this time on a larger scale. It was headed by a charismatic figure called Bar Kochba and supported by the revered Rabbi Akiba.

Bar Kochba inspired his followers to victory and for three years they were able to maintain their own sovereignty. They succeeded in taking Jerusalem and even minted their own coins. However, all their dedication and determination could not make up for their physical weakness. They simply could not withstand the great forces of Rome. The Bar Kochba rebellion was crushed in 135 but the participants had inflicted such heavy losses upon the Romans that Emperor Hadrian, in his report to the Senate, was forced to omit the usual formula: "I and the army are well."

The disaster brought on by Bar Kochba's defeat was tremendous. The Talmud states: "for 52 years no fowl was seen flying in the Land of Israel" (Taanit). The Romans built a new city on the site of Jerusalem — they called it Aelia Capitolina — and forbade Jews to approach it on pain of death. Once a year, on Tisha B'Av, Jews streamed to the sacred site to lament their loss, bribing Roman guards to permit them to linger and weep. Hadrian then attempted to eradicate Judaism by prohibiting circumcision, observance of the Sabbath, and teaching Torah. The rabbis boldly defied the decrees with the result that many met a cruel martyr's death, including the venerable Rabbi Akiba.

Once again, the resilience of the Palestinian Jewish community was revealed and the people engaged in rebuilding. Judea lay in ruins but not the Galilee where fighting had not occurred. The authority of the Nasi was whittled down so that the office existed in name only. The situation became more difficult after 364 when the Roman Empire split into two, one half being centered in Rome and the other in Constantinople (Byzantium). Palestine was under the sovereignty of the latter. Under the Byzantines, the economic hardships were so oppressive that many Jews found life impossible and had to leave. They migrated to Babylonia or to other parts of the Empire. From the middle of the sixth century on, the Jews were a minority in their own land — but a substantial one that never vanished altogether.

When the Persians took Palestine from the Byzantines in 614, the Jews had cause for hope. They were promised dominion over Jerusalem and even had reason to expect autonomy. The Persians, however, violated the agreement they had made with the Jews. Yet their rule was so short that one cannot judge what might have happened had they not been routed after 15 years by the returning Byzantines who were able to retake Palestine briefly.

By then, however, both the Persians and the Byzantines had so exhausted themselves that they could not withstand the new, energetic force emerging from the Arabian peninsula, the army of Islam. Palestine had suffered greatly from the armies that had traversed the country; many cities were abandoned because the inhabitants had taken to the hills; agriculture had come to a standstill; much of Jerusalem was in ashes.

Discussion Questions

1) There are people who believe that it is the duty of every Jew to leave the Diaspora (galut) and move to Israel. What did the rabbis have to say on the subject? Since we live in galut how should we respond to the Rabbis? Could you ever see yourself living in Israel? Why/why not?

2) According to rabbinic thought, should you plan to spend some time studying in Israel? What are your plans?

3) Based on the source Sotah 14a, near the beginning of this chapter, can you think of some mitzvot that can only be performed in the land of Israel? Why do you think there are mitzvot which can only be performed in Israel?

RELIGIOUS POETRY

If one were asked where to turn in order to learn what the Rabbis taught, the person would be directed to the Talmud and Midrash. Then, one would have to add: the Jewish prayerbook, the *siddur*, as well. Not because the Rabbis wrote or edited the *siddur* we use today, but because they did create the foundations of Jewish liturgy. They recognized that people needed to find ways to come close to God. As long as the Temple stood, they had done so primarily by offering sacrifices. Once the Temple disappeared, prayer became the substitute for the sacrificial system. The Rabbis proceeded to structure the Jewish worship service.

This service was never a static one. The essential core was rabbinic but new expressions of religious faith were incorporated in subsequent generations. The *siddur* thus included Biblical passages (e.g., the *Shma* and various psalms), rabbinic compositions, and works by inspired poets of various ages. It was the embodiment of Jewish aspirations, dreams and values. Whoever seeks to know what all Jews — scholars or unlearned, rich or poor, leaders or followers —

believed, thought, cared most about, must turn to the *siddur*.

It contains the entire gamut of human experience: prayers for weekdays, Sabbaths and Festivals in the morning, afternoon and evening; what is said before eating and what is said after eating; the rites for naming a child, a marriage, one's last moments, funeral and burial; songs *(zemirot)*; ethics *(Pirkei Avot)*; blessings for all occasions; individual and collective memories, desires and aspirations. The *siddur*, more than any other work reflects the dreams, philosophy and theology of Judaism. Prof. Robert Gordis has aptly referred to it as "the treasure house of Israel's faith to which every generation has brought its choicest gifts of aspiration and hope."

There is hardly a page without mention of Zion or Jerusalem. In the early part of the morning service, the worshipper is reminded:

The Lord has chosen Zion, he desired it for His dwelling place!	כִּי־בָחַר יְיָ בְּצִיּוֹן אִוָּהּ לְמוֹשָׁב לוֹ:

This is soon followed by:

the Lord rebuilds Jerusalem, gathers the dispersed. ... Jerusalem, Praise the Lord. Sing to your God, Zion. (Psalms 147)	בּוֹנֵה יְרוּשָׁלַיִם יְיָ; נִדְחֵי יִשְׂרָאֵל יְכַנֵּס. שַׁבְּחִי, יְרוּשָׁלַיִם, אֶת יְיָ; הַלְלִי אֱלֹהַיִךְ, צִיּוֹן.

The second paragraph of the Shma is a quotation from chapter 11 of the Book of Numbers which asserts the concept of Reward and Punishment, the idea that following the word of God bring benefits while rejecting it causes disaster. In this section, it is phrased in physical terms for the people. Goodness will result in the land being fertile, the "land" being the Land of Israel. Disobedience will result in famine and exile "from the good land which the Lord is giving you," that "land" also being the Land of Israel. Moreover, the reward for *tefillin* is clearly stated:

Then your days and the days of your children on the land which the Lord swore to give to your ancestors will endure as the days of the heavens over the earth.	לְמַעַן יִרְבּוּ יְמֵיכֶם וִימֵי בְנֵיכֶם עַל הָאֲדָמָה אֲשֶׁר נִשְׁבַּע יְהֹוָה לַאֲבֹתֵיכֶם לָתֵת לָהֶם כִּימֵי הַשָּׁמַיִם עַל־ הָאָרֶץ:

The Jew prays three times a day; morning, afternoon and evening. Each of those services is designated by its own name respectively: *shacharit, mincha,* and *maariv.* In all three, a collection of nineteen blessings called the *amidah* is recited. Thus, throughout the ages, nearly every Jew prays three times a day:

Have mercy, Lord, and return to Jerusalem, Your city. May Your Presence dwell there as You have promised. Build it now, in our days and for all time. Reestablish there the majesty of David, Your servant. Praised are You, Lord, who builds Jerusalem.	וְלִירוּשָׁלַיִם עִירְךָ בְּרַחֲמִים תָּשׁוּב, וְתִשְׁכּוֹן בְּתוֹכָהּ כַּאֲשֶׁר דִּבַּרְתָּ, וּבְנֵה אוֹתָהּ בְּקָרוֹב בְּיָמֵינוּ בִּנְיַן עוֹלָם, וְכִסֵּא דָוִד לְתוֹכָהּ תָּכִין. בָּרוּךְ אַתָּה יְיָ, בּוֹנֵה יְרוּשָׁלָיִם.

45

A few paragraphs later, the prayer concludes:

May we witness your merciful וְתֶחֱזֶינָה עֵינֵינוּ בְּשׁוּבְךָ
return to Zion. לְצִיּוֹן בְּרַחֲמִים.

This is recited as part of every *amidah;* the prayer above, *uvnei Yerushalayim,* is recited only on weekdays. Bearing that in mind, the longing of all Jewry and especially of many of Soviet Jews can be appreciated from this story. A USY alumna visited the Moscow synagogue with another woman with whom she toured. They went there Shabbat morning and were directed to sit in the back. One of the men up front got up to greet them but was told to take his seat. A few minutes later, he picked up a *siddur* to give to the guests and was permitted to do so. He opened the book, ostensibly to show them the place. But he had opened it to the weekday *amidah* and, as he handed over the prayerbook, he put his finger on "*uvnei Yerushalayim*", rebuild Jerusalem!"

On Sabbath and Festival mornings, an additional *amidah* is recited. It is called "*musaf.*" The *musaf* of *Yomtov* offers an explanation of why Jews were no longer in Zion. Neither Rome nor any other enemy was blamed. The answer it gives is: "*Mipnei hataeinu galinu mei-artzeinu,* "Because of our sins were we exiled from our land." If only our ancestors had adhered to the covenant and followed God's ways, they would not have been separated from their land which was an integral part of the *brit,* the covenant between God and His people. The recitation of this prayer is a call to obey the commandments and an expression of the hope that a reconciliation can indeed be effected, a reconciliation that includes a Return.

The *musaf* of *Shabbat* voices the prayer that Jews will be helped by God go to *Eretz Yisrael* and settle therein.

Every occasion evokes an opportunity to express the Jew's love for Zion. In chanting the *berakhot* (blessings) that follow the prophetic reading each Shabbat *(haftarah)*, the honoree says:

Show compassion for Zion, the fount of our existence. And bring hope soon to the humbled spirit. Praised are you, Lord, who brings joy to Zion.

רַחֵם עַל־צִיּוֹן כִּי הִיא
בֵּית חַיֵּינוּ וְלַעֲלוּבַת
נֶפֶשׁ תּוֹשִׁיעַ בִּמְהֵרָה
בְיָמֵינוּ. בָּרוּךְ אַתָּה יְיָ,
מְשַׂמֵּחַ צִיּוֹן בְּבָנֶיהָ:

The religious individual recognized that food should not be taken for granted, that it is a gift for which one should thank God. Thus the *birkat hamazon* (Grace after meals) was instituted. And, while thanking God for food, Zion is remembered.

Lord our God, have mercy for Your People Israel, Jerusalem Your city, Zion the home of Your glory, the kingdom of the House of David Your anointed and the great and holy House which is called by Your name. Fully rebuild Jerusalem the holy city, soon in our time. Praised are You, Lord, who in His mercy rebuilds Jerusalem. Amen.

רַחֵם יְיָ אֱלֹהֵינוּ עַל־
יִשְׂרָאֵל עַמֶּךָ, וְעַל
יְרוּשָׁלַיִם עִירֶךָ, וְעַל
צִיּוֹן מִשְׁכַּן כְּבוֹדֶךָ, וְעַל
מַלְכוּת בֵּית דָּוִד
מְשִׁיחֶךָ, וְעַל־הַבַּיִת
הַגָּדוֹל וְהַקָּדוֹשׁ שֶׁנִּקְרָא
שִׁמְךָ עָלָיו: וּבְנֵה
יְרוּשָׁלַיִם עִיר הַקֹּדֶשׁ
בִּמְהֵרָה בְיָמֵינוּ, בָּרוּךְ
אַתָּה יְיָ, בֹּנֶה בְרַחֲמָיו
יְרוּשָׁלָיִם, אָמֵן:

Many people, since the fifth of Iyar, May 15, 1948, insert a special prayer that the Merciful One (*Harahaman*) will bless the State of Israel and guard it from harm. Also, many synagogues on *Shabbat* morning now add the prayer for the State of Israel after reciting the prayer for the country in which we are living. By incorporating this prayer we show that not only are we attached and loyal to the land in which we live, we are also attached and loyal to Israel. Just as there are special prayers on Hanukkah and Passover reflecting our gratitude for the miraculous deeds wrought by God on those days *(al hanissim)*, so too newer editions of the prayerbook (e.g. *Sim Shalom*) include an *al hanissim* for Israel Independence Day *(Yom HaAtzma'ut)*.

Because Jews feel that *Eretz Yisrael* is their national home and Jerusalem the holy city, they pray turning toward them. In Western Europe, everyone turns eastward; the Ark containing the Torah scrolls is placed on the eastern wall. Jews who live east of Jerusalem, on the other hand, turn westward when they pray. In Israel, worshippers turn toward Jerusalem; in Jerusalem, they face the Temple Mount.

When a bride and groom stand under the marriage canopy, blessings are chanted praising God. One of them reads:

May Zion rejoice as her children return to her in joy. We praise You, Lord, who causes Zion to rejoice in her children.	שׂוֹשׂ תָּשִׂישׂ וְתָגֵל הָעֲקָרָה, בְּקִבּוּץ בָּנֶיהָ לְתוֹכָהּ בְּשִׂמְחָה, בָּרוּךְ אַתָּה יְיָ, מְשַׂמֵּחַ צִיּוֹן בְּבָנֶיהָ:

The service is concluded by the bridegroom

breaking a glass, that is a memorial of the destruction of Jerusalem and the Temple.

Even when someone dies, the mourner is consoled with words associated with his people's historic loss. The tradition is to greet the mourners in their home during *shiva* (the seven days of mourning) and on Friday evening in the synagogue, after the *lekha dodi* poem, with the words:

"May God comfort you together with all the other mourners of Zion and Jerusalem."

הַמָּקוֹם יְנַחֵם אֶתְכֶם בְּתוֹךְ שְׁאָר אֲבֵלֵי צִיּוֹן וִירוּשָׁלָיִם:

If it is possible, a little bag of Holy Land earth is placed beneath the head of the deceased before burial.

On Sabbath, special songs *(zemirot)* are sung by the participants in the Shabbat meal as they leisurely sit at the table. The *zemirot* extol the Sabbath and God who gave it to Israel as a most precious gift. They, too, express the great love of Zion.

Return to Your sanctuary and the Holy of Holies. The place where all feel joy, Where lovely songs will be rendered In Jerusalem the city of splendor.

(Yah Ribon)

לְמִקְדָּשָׁךְ תּוּב וּלְקֹדֶשׁ קֻדְשִׁין, אֲתַר דִּי בֵהּ יֶחֱדוּן רוּחִין וְנַפְשִׁין, וִיזַמְּרוּן שִׁירִין וְרַחֲשִׁין, בִּירוּשְׁלֵם קַרְתָּא דִי־שֻׁפְרַיָּא:

Have mercy, O God, for your people, For the site of Your

רַחֵם בְּחַסְדָּךְ, עַל עַמָּךְ צוּרֵנוּ, עַל צִיּוֹן מִשְׁכַּן

splendor, Zion, which we pray will be fully restored. May David's descendant redeem us, Anointed of the Lord.	כְּבוֹדֶךָ, זְבוּל בֵּית תִּפְאַרְתֵּנוּ, בֶּן־דָּוִד עַבְדֶּךָ, יָבֹא וְיִגְאָלֵנוּ, רוּחַ אַפֵּינוּ, מְשִׁיחַ יְיָ:

(Tzur Mishelo)

The *haggadah*, read at the Passover *seder*, was once part of the prayerbook but subsequently became a separate book because of the ease of holding a smaller work. At the very beginning of the *seder*, it is announced: "Now we are here. Next year in the land of Israel. (*Hashata hakha, Leshanah habaah bear'a deyisrael*)." The story of the Exodus from Egypt is told and verses of the Torah are discussed, the meal is eaten and the special songs are sung, and the *seder* is concluded with the ardent prayer: "*Lashanah Habaah Byrushalayim*, Next year in Jerusalem!"

It is of interest to note that many Jews have added a fifth cup of wine to the traditional four since the State of Israel was born. The four cups represent four expressions of redemption used in the Torah in relating the event of Egypt:

וְהוֹצֵאתִי — "And I shall bring you forth"

וְהִצַּלְתִּי — "I will deliver you from bondage"

וְגָאַלְתִּי — "I will redeem you"

וְלָקַחְתִּי — "I will take you"

(Exodus 6:6-7)

There is an additional expression in the following verse:

וְהֵבֵאתִי — "I will bring you in the Land"

No fifth cup of wine was assigned to represent

that promise. Perhaps, since the *seder* practices were developed by the rabbis who lived after the Destruction of the year 70, when the loss of freedom in the Land was so deeply felt, it was considered inappropriate. Perhaps it was hoped that it would be introduced when independence would be attained. Nevertheless, Rabbi Menachem Kasher, in his edition of the *haggadah*, points to the Talmudic passage (Talmud Bavli, Pesahim 118a): "Our sages have taught: For the fifth cup one recites *hallel hagadol;* these are the words of Rabbi Tarphon." Rabbi Kasher continues to cite the statement of Rabbi Sherira Gaon: "And there are those who say that four cups indicate four periods of exile, and the fifth cup indicates salvation" (p. 170). Many Jews look upon the establishment of the State of Israel as the beginning of a new era, one that will lead to Redemption, and therefore add a fifth cup of wine before concluding the *seder.*

The poetry of the Golden Age in Spain reached its peak in the work of Yehudah Halevi (1086 - ca 1141), the "sweet singer of Zion." When Halevi was born, Spain was divided into two: the Christian North and Moslem South. He was born in Toledo, which was under the Christians, went to school in the South and then returned home to practice medicine. He was not satisfied with the lack of cultured men of his own kind and accordingly moved to Cordoba where there were many Jewish scholars. A contemporary, Moses ibn Ezra, wrote that Yehudah Halevi was "a star come forth from Castile destined to illuminate the world."

In his poems, Yehudah Halevi was indeed Zion's harp. (Many today are moved by the song written by Naomi Shemer, "*Yerushalayim Shel Zahav.*" In that popular song, the poetess sings: "I am a harp for your songs! *ulekhal shirayikh ani kinor.*" These words were borrowed from Halevi). In eloquent and passionate verses, he gave expression to his people's deepest yearnings. In his younger days, Halevi wrote secular as well as religious poetry but his songs of love and friendship pale in comparison with his Zionides and his songs of God. More than three hundred of his poems have been incorporated into the liturgy. On Tisha B'Av, when the destruction of Zion is mourned by fast and prayer, Halevi's "Ode To Zion" is recited with loving emotion. In words that have become immortal, Yehudah Halevi caught the longing of his brethren for Jerusalem and *Eretz Yisrael*.

ODE TO ZION
צִיּוֹן הֲלֹא תִשְׁאֲלִי

SELECTED

Zion! wilt thou not ask if peace be with thy captives That seek thy peace — that are the remnant of thy flocks?	צִיּוֹן הֲלֹא תִשְׁאֲלִי לִשְׁלוֹם אֲסִירַיִךְ דֹּרְשֵׁי שְׁלוֹמֵךְ וְהֵם יֶתֶר עֲדָרָיִךְ׃
From west and east, from north and south — the greeting "Peace" from far and near, take thou from every side.	מִיָּם וּמִזְרָח וּמִצָּפוֹן וְתֵימָן שְׁלוֹם רָחוֹק וְקָרוֹב שְׂאִי מִכֹּל עֲבָרָיִךְ׃
To wail for thine affliction I am like the jackals; but when I dream Of the return of thy captivity, I am a harp for thy songs.	לִבְכּוֹת עֱנוּתֵךְ אֲנִי תַנִּים. וְעֵת אֶחֱלֹם שִׁיבַת שְׁבוּתֵךְ אֲנִי כִנּוֹר לְשִׁירָיִךְ׃
Thou are the house of royalty; thou art the throne of the Lord, and how Do slaves sit	אַתְּ בֵּית מְלוּכָה וְאַתְּ כִּסֵּא אֲדֹנָי. וְאֵיךְ יָשְׁבוּ

now upon thy princes'
thrones? Would I might be
wandering in the places where
God was revealed unto thy
seers and messengers.
O who will make me wings,
that I may fly afar,
And lay the ruins of my cleft
heart among thy
broken cliffs!
I would fall, with my face
upon thine earth and take
delight In thy stones and be
tender to thy dust.
I would pass into thy forest
and thy fruitful field, and
stand Within thy Gilead, and
wonder at thy mount beyond
— Zion! perfect in beauty!
love and grace thou didst bind
on thee of olden time; and still
the soul of thy companions
are bound up with thee.
It is they that rejoice at thy
well-being, that are in pain
over thy desolation, and that
weep over thy ruin.
Thy God hath desired thee for
a dwelling-place; and happy is
the man Whom He chooseth
and bringeth near that he may
rest within thy courts.

עֲבָדִים עֲלֵי כִסְאוֹת
גְּבִירָיִךְ:
מִי-יִתְּנֵנִי מְשׁוֹטֵט
בַּמְּקוֹמוֹת אֲשֶׁר נִגְלוּ
אֱלֹהִים לְחוֹזַיִךְ וְצִירָיִךְ:
מִי יַעֲשֶׂה-לִּי כְנָפַיִם
וְאַרְחִיק נְדֹד אָנִיד
לְבִתְרֵי לְבָבִי בֵּין
בְּתָרָיִךְ:
אֶפֹּל לְאַפִּי עֲלֵי אַרְצֵךְ
וְאֶרְצֶה אֲבָנַיִךְ מְאֹד
וַאֲחֹנֵן אֶת-עֲפָרָיִךְ:
אֶעֱבֹר בְּיַעְרֵךְ וְכַרְמִלֵּךְ
וְאֶעֱמֹד בְּגִלְעָדֵךְ
וְאֶשְׁתּוֹמְמָה אֶל-הַר
עֲבָרָיִךְ:
צִיּוֹן כְּלִילַת יֹפִי אַהֲבָה
וְחֵן תִּקְשְׁרִי מֵאָז. וּבָךְ
נִקְשְׁרוּ נַפְשׁוֹת חֲבֵרָיִךְ:
הֵם הַשְּׂמֵחִים לְשַׁלְוָתֵךְ
וְהַכֹּאֲבִים עַל-שְׁמָמוֹתֵךְ
וּבֹכִים עַל-שִׁבְרָיִךְ: אַוָּךְ
לְמוֹשָׁב אֱלֹהָיִךְ.
וְאַשְׁרֵי-אֱנוֹשׁ יִבְחַר
יְקָרֵב וְיִשְׁכֹּן בַּחֲצֵרָיִךְ:

Thus, at every occasion of prayer, in the
synagogue and in the home, on nearly every page of
the prayerbook, the Jews remembered Zion with a
love that defied time and geography. As Rabbi Israel

Levinthal (the great American Conservative rabbi) once wrote:

> The Jew, even though he was driven from the land, never surrendered his love for it.... The Jew literally transplanted Palestine into his very consciousness....In whatever clime he lived, he was always under the illusion that he was still in his ancient home. His very name Jew was a living protest that he still held his lien upon the land of Judea, from which, though he was torn physically, he was never separated in heart or mind. He sang of Palestine, dreamed of Palestine; it was uppermost in his thoughts in time of supremest joy and darkest sorrow.
>
> (*Judaism*, pp. 249-250)

Discussion Questions

1) After reading this chapter, how do you feel knowing that in almost every prayer you recite the land of Israel is mentioned? Do you agree with those prayers? Why/why not?

2) Compare and contrast the prayer for the country in which you live and the prayer for the State of Israel. Is one more spiritual than the other? What are the different things for which we are praying? Which one do you feel more comfortable reciting? Why?

3) Do you think the thrice daily recitations of these prayers would have motivated the various *aliyah* movements mentioned in chapter IV?

Chapter 4

ALIYOT

At various moments in history, individuals (such as Yehuda Halevi or Nachmanides) or groups of people decided that dreaming was not enough and that going to *Eretz Yisrael* was an imperative. There was no mass *aliyah* (going up to Zion) as there has been in the twentieth century but there was indeed *aliyah* from time to time.

Halevi felt that he was in Jerusalem even while still in Spain. There was no question in his mind that he would go there.

MY HEART IS IN THE EAST
לִבִּי בְמִזְרָח

My heart is in the east, and I in the utter-most west— How can I find savour in food? How shall it be sweet to me? How shall I render my vows and my bonds, while yet Zion lieth	לִבִּי בְמִזְרָח וְאָנֹכִי בְּסוֹף מַעֲרָב אֵיךְ אֶטְעֲמָה אֶת אֲשֶׁר־אֹכַל וְאֵיךְ יֶעֱרַב אֵיכָה אֲשַׁלֵּם נְדָרַי וֶאֱסָרַי בְּעוֹד צִיּוֹן בְּחֶבֶל אֱדוֹם וַאֲנִי בְּכֶבֶל עֲרָב יֵקַל בְּעֵינַי עֲזֹב כָּל־טוּב

55

beneath the fetter of Edom, and I in Arab chains? A light thing would it seem to me to leave all the good things of Spain — Seeing how precious in mine eyes it is to behold the dust of the desolate sanctuary.

סְפָרַד כְּמוֹ יַקַר בְּעֵינַי רְאוֹת

עַפְרוֹת דְּבִיר נֶחֱרָב:

Halevi was not one to preach without acting. As a middle-aged man, he resolved to undertake the difficult journey to Zion even though it meant leaving his only daughter and beloved grandson. He first went to Egypt where he stopped a while. His many friends urged him to remain, warning him of the many dangers that lay ahead. He, however, was determined to stand at the gates of Jerusalem. Legend has it that, that is when Yehudah Halevi came to his "Ode to Zion" *(tziyon halo tishali)*. While saying the words, an Arab horseman rode by and put a spear in the poet's back. Thus, Halevi died with a song of Zion on his lips.

One of the giants of all Jewish history was Rambam, Rabbi Moses ben Maimon, Maimonides (1135-1204). His eminence was such that a popular saying held that he was the greatest teacher since Moses: "From Moshe to Moshe, no one has arisen like Moshe מִמּשֶׁה לְמשֶׁה לֹא קָם כְּמשֶׁה." Maimonides was born in Spain and, when fanatical Moslems took the city, went with his family to Fez (in North Africa). Six years later, the family went to *Eretz Yisrael*. Unfortunately, conditions were so dangerous that they stayed only one year and left to settle in Egypt. There, Maimonides became the court physician. As the years passed, he not only served as rabbi but wrote many works. Each of his three major ones took ten years to complete: *Commentary to the Mishna; Mishneh Torah* (Code of Jewish Law); *Guide to the Perplexed*, an examination of religion from the point of view of philosophy.

Maimonides always regarded *Eretz Yisrael* as central. He taught:

It is forbidden ever to leave *Eretz Yisrael* unless it is to study Torah, to marry or to save one from enemies. And then the person should return. So one who leaves for business. But it is forbidden to live outside the Land unless food becomes unbearably expensive. ... Even though it be permissible to leave (for such a reason), it is not the pious thing to do. ...

Our sages said: The sins of one who lives in *Eretz Yisrael* are forgiven.

(Hilkhot Melakhim, Chapter 5)

אָסוּר לָצֵאת מֵאֶרֶץ יִשְׂרָאֵל לְחוּצָה לָאָרֶץ לְעוֹלָם. אֶלָא לִלְמוֹד תּוֹרָה אוֹ לִישָׂא אִשָׁה אוֹ לְהַצִּיל מִן הָעַכּוּ"ם וְיַחֲזוֹר לָאָרֶץ. וְכֵן יוֹצֵא הוּא לִסְחוֹרָה. אֲבָל לִשְׁכּוֹן בְּחוּצָה לָאָרֶץ אָסוּר אֶלָא אִם כֵּן חָזַק שָׁם הָרָעָב עַד שֶׁנַּעֲשָׂה שָׁוֶה דִינָר חִטִין בִּשְׁנֵי דִינָרִין. אָמְרוּ חֲכָמִים כָּל הַשּׁוֹכֵן בְּאֶרֶץ יִשְׂרָאֵל עֲוֹנוֹתָיו מְחוּלִין.

Maimonides felt guilty for remaining in Egypt and personally not returning. When he died, his body was taken to Tiberias for burial.

The outstanding Jewish personality of thirteenth century Spain was Rabbi Moshe ben Nachman,

Nachmanides (ca 1195 - ca 1270). Also a physician, he was a brilliant Bible scholar, Talmudist and philosopher. The historian, Graetz, observed: "The Talmud was for him all in all; in its light, he regarded the world, the events of the past and the shaping of the future."

In 1263, Nachmanides was ordered to take part in a public debate in Barcelona, in the presence of the King of Aragon. He had to defend Judaism against a convert to Christianity who was certain that he could prove that Jesus was the Messiah. Nachmanides was so successful that he was expelled from the country. Within a few years, he was able to leave Europe and settle in Jerusalem. There, he completed his most important work, his commentary on the Torah.

Nachmanides believed that it was a positive divine commandment for Jews to return to *Eretz Yisrael* and to settle there even before the final redemption. When they do the will of God, the widest possible borders will be restored.

Rabbi Nachman found the country desolate. In a letter written to his son after his arrival in Jerusalem in 1267 he wrote that "the more sacred the places, the greater their desolation. Jerusalem is more desolate than the rest of the country. Judea more than Galilee." Despite that, he could conclude: "It is a blessed land." When he arrived, he found a bare *minyan* that held services at their homes.

But we encourage them and we succeeded in finding a vacant house, built on pillars of marble with a beautiful arch. That we took for a synagogue. For the town is without a master, and whoever will take possession of the ruins can do so. We gave our offerings towards the repairs of the house.

(Schechter, *Studies in Judaism*, First Series, p. 108)

Rabbi Nachman proceeded to inform his son that people were continually coming to the city and was certain that "He who thought us unworthy to let us see Jerusalem in her desertion, He shall bless us to behold her again, built and restored, when the glory of the Lord will return unto her." Elsewhere, Nachmanides wrote of the longing for his family, yet:

But the loss of all this and of every other glory my eyes saw is compensated by having now the joy of being a day in thy courts (O Jerusalem), visiting the ruins of the Temple and crying over the ruined Sanctuary, where I am permitted to caress thy stones, to fondle thy dust, and to weep over thy ruins. I wept bitterly but I found joy in my tears. I tore my garments, but I felt relieved by it.

(*ibid*, pp.109-110)

With Nachmanides, the Jewish community began to develop anew.

In the early thirteenth century, life for Jews in France and England became increasingly more miserable. Pope Innocent III in Rome censured the French king, who tortured and plundered the Jews, for not being strict enough with those who had "murdered" their savior. Three hundred rabbis from France and England decided to leave Europe and go to the Land of the Fathers. They went to Jerusalem and built synagogues but they were unable to establish an on-going community.

In 1488, one of the great Italian scholars made *aliyah:* Rabbi Obadiah of Bartenura, noted for his commentary on the Mishna. He settled in Jerusalem, determined to change the appalling situation he found. In a letter to his father he wrote:

> I earnestly entreat that you will not be depressed nor suffer anxiety on account of my having travelled so far away, and that you will not shed tears for my sake. For God in His mercy has brought me to His holy dwelling, which rejoices my heart and should also delight you. God is my witness that I have forgotten all my former sorrows, and all remembrances of my native country have passed away from me. All the memories which I still retain of it are centered in your image, revered father, which is constantly before my eyes.
>
> (Kobler, *A Treasury of Jewish Letters,*
> Vol. 1, pp. 305-309)

The real beginning of the modern Yishuv (Jewish settlement in *Eretz Yisrael)* began after the expulsion of the Jews from Spain in 1492. The Jewish population grew quickly. Rabbis and scholars, the great luminaries of Spain and Portugal, came, often accompanied by members of their communities. Jerusalem, where Obadiah had hardly found a *minyan* ten years before, soon had thousands of Jews. There were flourishing settlements in Tiberias and Hebron while Safed became one of the most important Jewish centers in the world.

R. Joseph Karo (1488-1575), author of the *Shulkhan Aruch*, wrote: "After nearly fifteen hundred years of living in the exile and persecution, God remembered unto His people His covenant with their fathers, and brought them back from their captivity, one of a city and two of a family, from the corners of the earth to the land of glory, and they all settled in the city of Safed, the desire of all lands" (quoted by Schechter, *Studies*, Second Series, P. 202).

The Jews in Safed established local industries, developed trade and revitalized land which had remained desolate since the Crusaders. They raised the intellectual standards to such a level that *Eretz Yisrael* became the center of the Jewish world. The influx of scholars was so great that, in 1538, Rabbi Jacob Berab concluded that the time had come to reestablish the Sanhedrin. He began by attempting to revive the ancient institution of *smikhah*, the kind of ordination bestowed on the rabbis of the Mishnah. Rabbi Jacob Berab gathered in Safed thirty of the most prominent scholars and had them ordain him. He then proceeded to bestow his *smikhah* on them.

Karo had arrived in Safed about 1536. By then, there were at least 1,000 Jewish families in the city and new immigrants continued to arrive. There was a German Jewish community as well as a Spanish one, although the latter was dominant. There are also references to a Portuguese synagogue as well as Italian and Greek ones. Each had its own *yeshivah* and spiritual leader, but it seems that there was some kind of general council made up of the rabbis and of others as well.

Karo was but one of a distinguished circle. One of his colleagues was R. Shlomo Alkabetz, composer of *"Lekhah Dodi"*, the poem with which all praying Jews receive the Sabbath. In personifying the Shabbat as a bride and a queen, the poet sang her praises and included Jerusalem as the recipient of the blessings.

מִקְדַּשׁ מֶלֶךְ עִיר — Holy city, majestic, banish your fears. Arise, emerge from desolate years. Too long have you dwelled in the valley of tears. He will restore you with mercy and grace.

מְלוּכָה, קוּמִי צְאִי

מִתּוֹךְ הַהֲפֵכָה. רַב לָךְ

שֶׁבֶת בְּעֵמֶק הַבָּכָא,

וְהוּא יַחֲמוֹל עָלַיִךְ

חֶמְלָה.

In the sixteenth century, an audacious attempt to revive the Yishuv (the Jewish community of *Eretz Yisrael*) was made in Tiberias, a city not very far from Safed. The "Practical Zionist" was Don Joseph Nasi, a Marrano from Portugal, who became a close adviser to Suleiman the Magnificent. In 1561, the Sultan gave him the ruins of Tiberias with several surrounding villages and the title: "Lord of Tiberias". Don Joseph issued a proclamation inviting Jews to come to settle in Tiberias and help rebuild the city. It seems that he wanted to create the nucleus of a semi-autonomous Jewish State. Don Joseph sent adequate funds to repair, restore and build. He provided ships for those willing to leave Europe to come to labor and to find refuge.

One community near Rome, Cori, seemed eager to take advantage of Don Joseph's offer.

When we heard all this we were overcome with joy...We gathered in the synagogue, a representative of each family in the community being present...and discussed our intention of leaving here and settling beneath the wings of God in Tiberias as desired by our Lord Don Joseph. And all of us, without exception, agreed to make the necessary arrangements for the journey. Surely it was the doing of God that he brought such help and relief to meet the needs of the poor community of Cori....

(Ackerman, *Out of Our People's Past*, p. 39)

It is unknown why the Jews of Cori were not able to settle in Tiberias. Nor why Jews of other places failed to come. There were tremendous difficulties and, although he never gave up hope, Don Joseph's plans did not materialize.

The father of Hassidism was a charismatic personality known as the Baal Shem Tov (or, the Besht). The Besht lived with his wife in the mountains, away from communal life, for many years. There the Lurianic Kabbalism in which he had been nurtured developed and he emerged with new mystic insights of his own. Teaching the sheer joy of loving God and the religiosity of expressing emotion even for the non-intellectual, he acquired disciples and began a movement. Seeking the heart of each individual, the Baal Shem Tov taught that every person has a role to play in God's plan for salvation.

Just as the Besht was concerned for individuals, so was he concerned for the Jews as a whole and yearned for national redemption. Eight years before he died, he wrote to his brother-in-law that he had long considered making *aliyah* and that he had not yet given up that hope.

God knows that I have not despaired of the trip	הַשֵּׁם יוֹדֵעַ שֶׁאֵין אֲנִי מְיָאֵשׁ עַצְמִי מִנְּסִיעָה לָאָרֶץ

to *Eretz Yisrael,* if that be His will, to be together with you.

יִשְׂרָאֵל, אִם יִהְיֶה רְצוֹן ד׳, לִהְיוֹת עִמְּךָ יָחַד.

It is told that he actually began the journey one winter and got as far as Constantinople. Something unknown happened there to cause him to return home rather than proceed.

The Baal Shem Tov's son, R. Baruch, sent one of his closest disciples to help Hasidim settle in *Eretz Yisrael.* R. Baruch did not hear from him for two years and he decided to send another disciple to find out how he was. The latter journeyed to Tiberias and, as he entered the city, he saw his colleague's wife publicly doing laundry. He understood that they must be very poor and he decided to leave before being seen, thus not embarrassing the *rebbetzin* (rabbi's wife). She, however, looked up, saw him, arose and said: "Rabbi, these clothes are not ours. They belong to others and we wash them for a price. But this is *Eretz Yisrael* and we accept with love its difficulties."

The only one of the classic teachers of Hassidism who succeeded in visiting the Land of Israel was the Besht's great-grandson, R. Nachman of Bratzlav. R. Nachman was convinced that

All of our holiness and sanctity and all of our Jewishness depends on *Eretz Yisrael.*

כָּל קְדוּשָׁתֵנוּ וְטָהֳרָתֵנוּ וְכָל יַהֲדוּתֵנוּ תָּלוּי בְּאֶרֶץ יִשְׂרָאֵל.

He believed that in that land alone was it possible to mount the ladder of holiness higher and higher. The day before *Pesach* in 1798, R. Nachman emerged from the *mikveh* and told his attendant: "This year I will definitely be in the Holy Land. " His wife and family tried to dissuade him from embarking on such a dangerous journey but he was adamant and would not be deterred.

> It is impossible without this. For most of me is already there, and the minority must follow the majority. I have set my heart on this journey to *Eretz Israel*. I know that I will find my way blocked with countless barriers, but as long as my soul is in me, I will do everything in my power to go.

> (*Rabbi Nachman's Wisdom,*
> Aryeh Kaplan Translation, p. 37)

After all, he had taught:

The level of holiness of *Eretz Yisrael* is mighty and awesome, so much so that the mind cannot grasp its sanctity for we see that the entire Torah, from beginning to end, praises *Eretz Yisrael*. Every promise made by God to Abraham, Isaac and Jacob concerned inheriting the land. The redemption and exodus from Egypt led by our master Moses was to be privileged to come to Eretz Yisrael....

מַעֲלַת וְשֶׁבַח קְדוּשַׁת אֶרֶץ
יִשְׂרָאֵל גָּדוֹל וְנוֹרָא מְאֹד עַד
שֶׁאִי אֶפְשָׁר לְשַׁעֵר בְּמוֹחַ כְּלָל
גּוֹדֶל מַעֲלָתֶהּ וְכֹּחַ קְדוּשָׁתָהּ
כַּאֲשֶׁר אָנוּ רוֹאִים שֶׁכָּל הַתּוֹרָה
כּוּלָהּ מֵרֹאשָׁהּ וְעַד סוֹפָהּ
מְלֵאָה מִשֶּׁבַח אֶרֶץ יִשְׂרָאֵל.
וְכָל הַהַבְטָחָה שֶׁהִבְטִיחַ ד'
יִתְבָּרֵךְ אֶת אֲבוֹתֵינוּ לְאַבְרָהָם
וּלְיִצְחָק וּלְיַעֲקֹב הָיָה הָעִיקָר
עַל יְרוּשַׁת הָאָרֶץ. וְכֵן כָּל
גְּאוּלַת וִיצִיאַת מִצְרַיִם עַל יְדֵי
מֹשֶׁה רַבֵּינוּ עָלָיו הַשָּׁלוֹם הַכֹּל
הָיָה כְּדֵי לִזְכּוֹת לָבֹא לָאָרֶץ

Therefore, if a person truly believes in the sanctity of *Eretz Israel*, he will certainly run or fly there with all his strength and nothing will prevent him.

יִשְׂרָאֵל. וּמִכָּל זֶה יְכוֹלִין לִרְאוֹת וּלְהָבִין מֵרָחוֹק מַעֲלַת הַזּוֹכֶה לֵישֵׁב בָּהּ וַאֲפִילוּ לֵילֵךְ בָּהּ רַק אַרְבַּע אַמּוֹת, וְעַל כֵּן אִם הָיָה הָאָדָם מַאֲמִין בֶּאֱמֶת בִּקְדוּשַׁת אֶרֶץ יִשְׂרָאֵל חֵלֶק מֵאַלְפֵי אֲלָפִים מִכְּמוֹ שֶׁהוּא בֶּאֱמֶת בְּוַודַּאי הָיָה בְּכָל כּוֹחוֹ וְלֹא הָיָה שׁוּם מוֹנֵעַ שֶׁיִּמְנָעֵהוּ.
(ס' נחל נובע, עמ' קעד)

In May of 1798, Rav Nachman set forth on his journey and arrived in Haifa on September 10th. Once he set foot on the soil of the Land, he said that he had attained everything. He later said: "The moment I walked four steps in the Holy Land I achieved my goal." He experienced a mystic exaltation that never left him.

That contact with the soil was all he needed and he was ready to return home as soon as Rosh Hashanah was over. However, there were *hasidim* in Safed and Tiberias who begged him to visit them. He reluctantly acquiesced and stayed until the spring. His attendant noted:

> While in the Holy Land, the Rebbe was constantly involved with Torah and prayer. Every day he would write down what he perceived in Torah.
> When the Rebbe spoke about this, he said, 'The difference between the understanding of the Torah in the Holy Land and elsewhere is like the difference between East and West.' (Kaplan, P. 93)

The rest of his life, Rav Nachman was spiritually in the Holy Land. It became part of his very being and he would say: "My place is only in *Eretz Yisrael.*" He would also say to himself:

All of the life that he had came only from his dwelling in *Eretz Yisrael* and every thought that he had came only as a result of that stay because the basic part of the mind and of wisdom is in *Eretz Yisrael.*

כָּל הַחַיִּים שֶׁיֵּשׁ לוֹ הוּא מְיִּשִׁיבָתוֹ בְּאֶרֶץ יִשְׂרָאֵל וְכָל מַחֲשָׁבָה דֵעָה שֶׁיֵּשׁ לוֹ הִיא רַק מִכֹּחַ יְשִׁיבָתוֹ בְּאֶרֶץ יִשְׂרָאֵל, כִּי עִיקַר הַמוֹחַ וְהַחָכְמָה הוּא בְּאֶרֶץ יִשְׂרָאֵל.

There are many sayings of R. Nachman's regarding the Land of Israel.

In *Eretz Yisrael* the bread is so tasty that it includes the best taste of all the foods in the world.

בְּאֶרֶץ יִשְׂרָאֵל הַלֶּחֶם מוּטְעָם כָּל כַּךְ עַד שֶׁנִּכְלֶלֶת בֶּן כָּל מְתִיקוֹת הַטְעָמִים שֶׁבְּכָל הַמַאֲכָלִים בָּעוֹלָם.

Whoever wants to be a Jew, that is to ascend from one rung to the next, cannot do so except through *Eretz Yisrael.*

מִי שֶׁרוֹצֶה לִהְיוֹת יְהוּדִי, דְּהַיְינוּ לֵילֵךְ מִדַּרְגָּא לְדַרְגָּא, אִי אֶפְשָׁר כִּי אִם עַל יְדֵי אֶרֶץ יִשְׂרָאֵל.

The love of *Eretz Yisrael* remained a part of Hassidism but most Hasidic leaders opposed the World Zionist Organization created by Theodor Herzl. They persisted in waiting for a Messiah sent by God to initiate the Return and Redemption, regarding human undertakings as defiance of God. Moreover, they found it difficult to accept the leadership of non-religious secularists. There nevertheless have been *hasidim*, including rebbes, who have made *aliyah* and are citizens of the State of Israel.

The greatest Talmudic authority in Germany in the thirteenth century was R. Meir of Rothenberg (1220-1293). Towards the end of his life, the situation of the Jews became unbearable. Knowing that the authorities were averse to the Jews leaving the country, R. Meir and his followers made secret plans to go to *Eretz Yisrael*. They left home in 1286 and began their journey. En route, however, an apostate recognized the renowned scholar and reported him to the bishop who had him seized. Upon the emperor's orders, R. Meir was imprisoned. The Jews raised large sums to buy his release but R. Meir refused. He did not want to set a precedent for taking hostages for ransom. He remained in prison for the rest of his life.

In a responsum (an answer to a question dealing with Jewish law; there is a vast literature of Jewish responsa), R. Meir rules that a father does not have the right to prevent his son from going to *Eretz Yisrael*. This a *mitzvah* that has priority over the *mitzvah* of honoring parents.

You ask whether the father is entitled to prevent his son from migrating to the Land of Israel. Because it is a mitzvah to go to the Land of Israel, as it is written "I am the Lord Your God," the son need not obey the father. For the honor of the Lord ranks above all.

(Kobler, p. 242)

When R. Meir was asked the meaning of the Talmudic statement: "A person who dwells in the Diaspora is as one who has no God," he responded: "God's presence is primarily concentrated in the Holy Land. Therefore, a person's prayers there ascend directly to His throne".

(Rabbi Meir of Rothenberg, Agus, p. 681)

In 1614, the Maharal was succeeded in the rabbinate of Prague by Rabbi Isaiah Hurvitz (ca 1555-1630), also known as "Sheloh" (initials of his great work: *Shnei Luhot Habrit,* The Two Tablets of the Covenant). The Sheloh was widely admired and highly respected. He was able to present Jewish teachings, Kabbalah as well, in a way that simple people could understand them.

He long desired to make *aliyah,* to study and to teach in Zion. In the mid-fifties, he carried out his intentions and settled in Jerusalem. In one of his letters to his children, after relating all that happened en route, he wrote:

Although Jerusalem lies in ruins now, it is still the glory of the whole earth. There is peace and safety, good food and delicious wine, all much cheaper than in Safed..... The Sephardim also increase very much in Jerusalem, even in the hundreds, and they build big houses there. We consider all this as a sign of deliverance, may it come speedily.

He went on to tell of his plans to teach and develop an important center of Torah studies in Jerusalem. And he continued:

My beloved children, tell everybody who intends to go to the Holy Land to settle in Jerusalem. Let nobody assume that I give this advice because I shall settle there. Far be this from me! But I give this advice in all sincerity because all good is there and nothing is lacking. The city is enclosed and surrounded by a wall. It is a big as Lwow, but the most important point is that it is particularly holy and the gate of heaven.

(Kobler, pp. 483-484)

In the eighteenth century there lived one of the greatest intellectuals of all Jewish history, the Gaon of Vilna (1720- 1797). It is reported that by the age of nine, he was well- versed in the entire Bible and Talmud; at ten, in the course of six months, he completed the entire Zohar; by twelve, he knew astronomy well. In addition to his mastery of all Jewish sources, the Gaon was in full command of algebra, geometry and trigonometry. He was also well-versed in medicine. Rabbi Solomon Schechter pointed out: "It must be understood that to learn Torah meant for the Gaon more than the brain work for the purpose of gaining knowledge. To him it was a kind of service to God." (*Studies in Judaism*, First Series, p. 85) Prof. Louis Ginzberg once noted that it would require more than dozen lectures to give an adequate estimate of the Gaon's phenomenal mentality and lasting contribution to the different branches of Jewish learning.

The Gaon taught that *Torah* and *Eretz Yisrael* are intertwined bases of Judaism. He often thought of going to Jerusalem and spoke with his disciples about the religious merit of settling there. Once, he actually made the move. He expected to strike roots and then bring his wife and family. En route, he wrote to them, beginning:

I am writing to you not to be upset at my leaving, as you have promised me you would not. Truthfully, what is there to worry about? People travel for years to make money, leaving their wives, travelling about with almost no personal belongings. I, thank God, am travelling to the Holy Land which all desire to see, the treasure of the Jewish people and of God himself.

For some unknown reason, the Gaon turned back after reaching Austria. There are some who think that, en route, he heard that the Hasidim dominated the Jewish communities of Palestine. The Gaon was an implacable opponent of Hassidism. But he did not want to disturb the peace of Jews living in the Holy Land and turned back rather than cause controversy among them. Some disciples of the Gaon who were also mystics believed that the reason for his return was that the Gaon has a spark of Moses' soul and, since Heaven had not permitted Moses to enter the Promised Land, so it deterred the Gaon. One of the disciples who had moved to Eretz Yisrael and was an old man when asked for an explanation of the Gaon not continuing, responded by quoting the Talmud (Sotah 14a).

Why did Moses so desire to enter Eretz Yisrael? Did he need to eat the fruit there or to enjoy its bounty? NO. This is what Moses thought: Israel was commanded many mitzvot (religious obligations) which could be carried out only in Eretz Yisrael. I want to enter the Land in order to fulfill those *mitzvot.*

He went on to assert that the Gaon was similarly motivated. Rabbi Yehuda Leib Maimon (the first Minister of Religions of the State of Israel) who asked the question, commented years later: "My question was naive and so was the answer." The Gaon longed to go there as he wrote in his letter: "all desire to see the Land which is God's treasure". He had expected to study in the very place where Rabbinic Judaism was created; he thought that he could make *Eretz Yisrael* into a center of Torah for all Jewry. The reason for turning back is a mystery but the Gaon remained disappointed the rest of his days.

He did however, influence others to do what he had not done himself. Ten years after the death of the Gaon, his disciple, R. Menachem Mendel of Shklov went to Jerusalem and laid the foundation for the Ashkenazic *Perushim,* those who studied the Gaon's teachings and sought to spread them. R. Menachem Mendel wrote:

> I never moved from his side. Wherever he walked, I walked; wherever he slept, I slept. He opened for me the gates of wisdom and told me precious things. I also listened to what he said to others and built buildings upon that. It was his influence together with that of my sainted fathers that brought me to the Holy Land. I settled in the holy city of Safed and established there, with God's help, schools full of books. That was not enough for me. I came to Jerusalem, the city holy to God and there too established synagogues and study halls.
>
> (*Sarei Hameyah* II, Maimon, p. 141)

Another disciple of the Gaon, R. Yisrael of Shklov, had studied with the Gaon for twenty years and said: "God gave me the privilege of being in the presence of the king." In his book, *Peiat Hashulhan*, R. Yisrael ruled:

Whoever has a father and a mother outside the Land and protests his leaving their place to go to *Eretz Yisrael* he is not obligated to listen to his parents in this matter.

(ibid.)

He, himself, together with his parents and a group of loyal followers, left Lithuania to settle in Jerusalem. He devoted himself to rebuilding ruins with great love and energy, strengthening the community of the Gaon's disciples.

Discussion Questions

1) If the government of Israel would completely fund your move to Israel, as Don Joseph was ready to do, would you be willing to go? Is money the only issue in your decision to make *aliyah*?

2) How would you feel if your community leaders (rabbis, educators, etc.) decided to make *aliyah*? Compare this chapter to Rabbi James Lebeau's article in the Winter 1988 issue of *Hamadrich*.

3) What attitude does Rabbi Meir of Rothenburg's statement on *aliyah* (viz. that the father cannot prevent the son from making *aliyah*) reflect? Do you agree with his statement? Why/why not?

4) What do you think a trip (let alone a move) to Israel entailed in the middle ages? Does the knowledge of what the trip entailed make the people who undertook the journey more righteous or more committed? Would that lessen the commitment of people who make *aliyah* today?

BENEFACTORS

In the early nineteenth century, the Jews in Palestine lived in one of the four "holy cities" (Jerusalem, Safed, Tiberias and Hebron) devoting themselves to prayer and study, depending on contributions from world Jewry to sustain themselves and their families. The beginnings of the modern *yishuv* did not take place until some Jews began to move out of the confines of their traditional locales and engage in work enabling them to earn a living. It took a man like Sir Moses Montefiore (1784-1885) to initiate the proceedings.

Montefiore was not a learned Jew in the world of religious practices and prayer. Throughout his life (and a long life it was, he almost reached his 101st birthday), he remained an ardent and committed Jew. At home and abroad, Sabbath and festival were carefully observed and dietary laws adhered to strictly. When the young Queen Victoria knighted him, his *kippah* was on his head.

Montefiore early achieved financial success as a broker on the London Stock Exchange and as founder of several business enterprises. He was so successful that he was able to retire from active business life at the age of 40 and devote the rest of his days to charitable and civic causes. As president of the Board of Deputies of British Jews, Montefiore was the spokesman for British Jewry and received requests for help form Jews throughout the world. He always responded generously and even travelled to Russia, Constantinople and Morocco to ease the plight of his brethren.

Montefiore's great love was for *Eretz Yisrael.* Despite the great discomforts and dangers of travel in his day, he went there seven times. He noted in the diary he kept on his last trip in 1875 that he undertook the journey "partly form the great attachment I ever felt toward the children of Zion and partly through the daily increasing interest which people of all different denominations appear now, more than ever, to evince in the welfare of Jerusalem". Even more, it was the Land itself which elicited his great love. The name of Jerusalem adorned his coat of arms and, on *Shabbat* and *Yomtov,* he wore a special ring on which Jerusalem was engraved.

There was no "Old City and "New City" before Moses Montefiore. He was responsible for building the first houses outside the wall surrounding Jerusalem. They constituted the first neighborhood of what is today "the New City"; its name is Mishkanot Shaanamim (or Yemin Moshe). On his 1875 trip, Montefiore was delighted to see those houses when he came to Jerusalem and he noted:

> Great was my delight when I considered that but a few years had passed since the time when one Jewish family was living outside the gate of Jerusalem — not a single house was to be seen; and now beheld almost a new Jerusalem springing in Europe.

"Surely", I exclaimed, "we are approaching the time to witness the realization of God's hallowed promise unto Zion!".

There are several other "firsts" to Sir Moses' credit. He was the first to have Jews plant orange groves, to establish a vocational school, to set up a printing press, and to build a windmill. Sir Moses was joined in his attachment to and efforts on behalf of *Eretz Yisrael* by his beloved wife, Judith. In her Journals, she related that one *Tisha B'Av*, before she was married, she and her sisters were in their drawing room dressed in mourning garb sitting on low stools. All of a sudden, the door opened and the maid entered followed by Admiral Sir Sidney Smith and a group of friends. The sisters were upset at being seen thus but Judith sat calmly. When the Admiral asked what happened, she told him:

> This is the day of remembering the destruction of Jerusalem. For all loyal Jews, this is a day of mourning and fasting. You and your honored friends no doubt know about the heroic deeds of our ancestors when fighting Rome and you will therefore understand our great sorrow that they were not able to save our holy city and the Temple from the Romans.

The Admiral responded: "The emotion which prompts every genuine patriot to grieve over his people's heroes who died fighting for their nation and their homeland is a noble and most exalted emotion. The memory of the battles which the Jews fought against the romans for the land given them by God will never be erased from the heart of every honest man in England".

(*Sarei Hameyah* V, Maimon, pp. 89-90).

On his 1855 trip, Sir Moses stopped in the home of one of the Jaffa notables. Though he had hurt his knee, "when the Minyan arrived for the Shabbat prayer, a ray of joy entered my heart, which became greatly enhanced by the reflection that God had permitted me again to celebrate that hallowed day in the Land of Promise."

At the end of his Diary, Sir Moses addressed his fellow Jews appealing to them for action.

In concluding this narrative I feel it my pleasing duty to inform all the friends of Zion, that the great regard which I always entertained towards our brethren in the Holy Land has now become; if possible, doubly increased, so that if your were to ask me, "Are they worthy and deserving of assistance" I would reply "Most decidedly.'
... If you put the question to me, saying thus: "Now we are willing to contribute to a fund intended to render them such assistance as they may require; we are ready to make even sacrifices of our own means if necessary; what schemes do you propose as best adopted to carry out simply what they themselves have suggested; but begin, in the first instance, with the building of houses in Jerusalem... .
... It is the amount of your fund be sufficient, build houses in Safed, Tiberias, and Hebron [the three other traditional holy cities]...

And if you now address me, saying "Which would be the proper time to commence the work, supposing we were ready to be guided by your counsel?" — My reply then would be: "Commence at once, begin the work this day, if you can."

A few years before he died, responding to someone who said it would be impossible to gather in the Holy Land all the Jews scattered over the globe, Sir Moses replied:

I do not expect that all the Israelites will quit their abodes in those territories in which they feel happy; but Palestine must belong to the Jews, and Jerusalem is destined to become the seat of a Jewish empire.

The great philanthropist who enabled the early *moshavot* (colonies) to take root and become the foundation of modern Israel was Baron Edmond de Rothschild (1845-1934). Rothschild, with all of his immense wealth never lost his commitment to the Jewish religion and to the Jewish people. For more than half a century, he not only contributed billions of francs to the Jewish settlements in Palestine, but gave most of his time as well. He left most of his business to his brothers and cousins while he was engaged in the work of the colonies. When he died, he was buried along with his wife in Zichron Yaakov (a community named in his memory which was built around his winery).

He once confided to one of his Zionist friends:

Everybody makes the mistake of assuming

that I joined the Palestine effort because I happened to see a couple of Jews from Russia. The truth is that I arrived at the idea much earlier when I observed the rapid strides of assimilation among the Jews of France, especially the mixed marriages. I saw great families, once the strongholds of Judaism, become estranged from us... I came to the conclusion that we must find a country where Judaism could develop further in the spirit of our great prophets. And I realized that the only place was Palestine where every plot of ground, every strip of soil, in town and in country, is saturated with the memories of the great eternal works of our prophets.

(Edmond de Rothschild, Naiditch, pp. 22-23)

The Baron was always ready to write out a check if convinced of a project's worthiness. When asked to help the Jewish schools in Palestine, he agreed as long as Jewish religious practices and traditions were respected. The "Father of the Yishuv" (as Baron de Rothschild is often called) did not always have an easy time in his work. Members of his family made fun of his interest and workers in his colonies often protested. The representatives of the Baron, who ran his various projects, often tried to complain to Baron Rothschild directly but he tended to back up the men whom he had appointed. Once, when he was upset because of complaints and seemingly petty quarrels in the *moshavot*, his wife (who shared his Jewish loyalties) said to him:

We have a tradition that *Eretz Yisrael* is acquired not only by money but by suffering. Those building the Land suffer greatly. With all their strength and energy, they are trying to revive the desolate land under the burning sun of Palestine or during heavy rains. They toil from early morning till dark. They have to plow and uproot, to fence ad to prune and to build — they suffer hunger and want. And, with all that, they have to stand guard to protect their lives and families from Arabs, thieves and murderers. And we? What do we suffer for *Eretz Yisrael?* ... The complaints and criticisms from certain circles, they are our suffering and through them we are privileged to revive our ancient land and rebuild it. We must accept such suffering with great love and be grateful to those who cause it, not become irate or upset.

(Lemaan Zion, Maimon, p. 151)

The Baron smiled, calmed down, and continued his work for Zion rebuilt.

Discussion Questions

1) Do you know of any present-day successors to Sir Moses Montefiore and Baron Edmund de Rothschild? Is it more or less difficult to be a "benefactor" of such magnitude today?

2) Is our responsibility to the state of Israel today any different than in the time of Montefiore and Rothschild? What do you think about the fact that Montefiore and Rothschild gave so much money to Israel but never settled in Israel? Would it have shown more commitment and sincerity had they lived

there? Would the same hold true for benefactors today?

3) Do you think Israel can survive without the support of the Diaspora? Jewish tourists from the Diaspora are looked down upon by the average Israeli because they think the only true means of support of Israel is making *aliyah*, not giving money. How would you respond to that average Israeli?

Chapter 6

RELIGION AND NATIONALISM: THE PRE-ZIONISTS

More than half a century before Theodor Herzl succeeded in gathering together an assembly of Jews to create the World Zionist Organization in 1897, there were individuals who came up with similar ideas. One of them was R. Yehudah Alkalai (1798-1878), a kabbalist who spent his childhood in Jerusalem and, in his late twenties, became rabbi of Zemun (near Belgrade). As early as 1834, Alkalai wrote a booklet proposing the creation of Jewish colonies in the Holy Land by the efforts of all Jews. In many subsequent books and pamphlets, he urged the establishment of settlements as the first step in redemption. He warned that the Messiah would not come unless Jews first undertook action to enable the development of Jewish settlements.

> We are, therefore, commanded not to attempt to go at once and all together to the Holy Land. In the first place, it is necessary for many Jews to remain for a time in the lands of dispersion, so that they can help the first settlers in Palestine, who will

undoubtedly come from among the poor. Secondly, the Lord desires that we be redeemed in dignity; we cannot, therefore, like Bedouins migrate in a mass, for we should then have to live like Bedouins, scattered in tents all over the fields of the Holy Land. Redemption must come slowly. The land must, by degrees, be built up and prepared....

(*Zionist Idea*, Hertzberg, p. 105)

Alkalai thought it possible to buy Palestine from the Turks and appealed to Montefiore and other notables to convoke a Great Assembly, to create a national fund to buy land, to float a national loan.

Alkalai objected to the idea of Jews emigrating to America. Once, after trouble in Rumania, the French organization to help Jews in distress, the *Alliance Israelite Universelle*, began to organize Jewish emigration across the Atlantic. Rabbi Alkalai wrote an open letter of protest:

In my humble opinion, the suggestion to send them to America is not a good one, to send them far from the roots of our holiness, from our Land, the inheritance of our forefathers. It cannot succeed because we would be causing distress to our Father in Heaven, who chose Jerusalem and to our holy fathers in Hebron (i.e. Abraham,	לְפִי קוֹצֶר דַּעְתִּי לֹא טוֹבָה הָעֵצָה הַיְעוּצָה לְשָׁלְחָם לְאַמֶּרִיקָה, לְהַרְחִיקָם וּלְהַתִּיקָם מִשּׁוֹרֶשׁ קְדֻשָּׁתֵנוּ מֵאַרְצֵנוּ וּמִנַחֲלַת אֲבוֹתֵינוּ, וְהִיא לֹא תִצְלַח כִּי בָה אָנוּ גוֹרְמִים צַעַר לְאָבִינוּ שֶׁבַּשָּׁמַיִם הַבּוֹחֵר בִּירוּשָׁלַיִם וּלְאֲבוֹתֵינוּ הַקְּדוֹשִׁים יְשֵׁנֵי חֶבְרוֹן וְרָחֵל אִמֵּנוּ לֹא תִמָּנַע קוֹלָהּ מִבֶּכִי. וְחַלִילָה לְחֶבְרַת

83

Isaac and Jacob): Mother Rachel would never cease weeping. Far be it from the *Alliance* to reject upon us to arouse us to return to Him and to gather in His house, to be faithful to His promise to those who are extremely asleep.....

The Lord will not pour gold dinars upon America, only toil and labor. But in our Holy Land it will also be possible to earn a living by the sweat of the brow, by hard work, for God has not abandoned the Land.

(Hadoar, 25 Iyyar 5714)

כָּל יִשְׂרָאֵל לִמְעוֹל מָעַל בְּה'.
וְאָבִינוּ שֶׁבַּשָּׁמַיִם הֵבִיא עָלֵינוּ
צָרוֹת רַבּוֹת וְרָעוֹת כְּדֵי
לְעוֹרֵר לְבָבֵנוּ לָשׁוּב אֵלָיו
יִתְבָּרַךְ וּלְהִסְתּוֹפֵף בְּבֵיתוֹ,
לְקַיֵּים אֱמוּנָתוֹ לִישֵׁינֵי
עָפָר. ...

לֹא יַמְטִיר ד' דִּינָרֵי זָהָב
בְּאַמֶרִיקָה כִּי אִם צָרִיךְ
עֲבוֹדָה וּמְלָאכָה, וְגַם
בְּאַרְצֵנוּ הַקְּדוֹשָׁה יוּכְלוּ
לְהִתְפַּרְנֵס, בְּזֵעַת אַפָּם
בַּעֲבוֹדָה וּמְלָאכָה כִּי עֲדַיִן
לֹא עָזַב ד' אֶת הָאָרֶץ.

(הדואר, כה' אייר, תשיד)

In 1872, Rabbi Alkalai settled in Jerusalem. He was active but he died a little known man.

A contemporary of Alkalai's was Rabbi Zvi Hirsch Kalisher, a renowned Talmudist and religious thinker who spent most of his rabbinic career in Thorn (once in Prussia, now Poland). While contemplating the compatibility of faith with reason, Kalisher began thinking about the redemption of the Jewish people and the coming of the Messiah. He concluded that the Messiah would not suddenly appear and then bring the Jews back to *Eretz Yisrael* through a miracle. Rather it was necessary for the Jews to settle the land and establish some form of government first. Only afterwards would the Messiah appear.

In 1862, Kalisher wrote a book entitled *Derishat Tziyon* (Seeking Zion). It was the first Hebrew book to appear on the subject of Modern Jewish agricultural settlement in Palestine. In it, the great scholar clearly set forth his views.

The redemption of Israel, for which we long, is not to be imagined as a sudden miracle. The Almighty, blessed be His Name, will not suddenly descend from on high and command His people to go forth.

He will not sent the Messiah from heaven in a twinkling of an eye, to sound the great trumpet for the scattered of Israel and gather them into Jerusalem. He will not surround the Holy City with a wall of fire or cause the Holy Temple to descend from the heavens. The bliss and the miracles that were promised by His servants, the prophets, will certainly come to pass — everything will be fulfilled — but we will not run in terror and flight, for the Redemption of Israel will come by slow degrees and the ray of deliverance will shine forth gradually.

My dear reader! Cast aside the conventional view that the Messiah will suddenly sound a blast on the great trumpet and cause all the inhabitants of the earth to tremble. On the contrary, the Redemption will begin by gaining the consent of the nations to the gathering of some of the scattered of Israel into the Holy Land....

(*The Zionist Idea*, pp. 111-112)

Rabbi Kalisher travelled through Germany hoping to convince wealthy Jews to contribute to Jewish settlement projects. He inspired the founding of several colonization societies. He was responsible for the establishment in 1864 of the Central Committee for Palestine Colonization in Berlin. Similar committees soon began to be formed elsewhere and they became the foundation of the *Hibbat Zion* movement (which preceded the World Zionist Organization). The rabbi of Thorn called for a Colonial Bank to raise money to buy land in Israel and for every Jew to further the cause of Jewish settlement.

Rabbi Kalisher wrote about the need to train young Jews in agriculture. He won the interest of the leaders of the *Alliance* who proceeded to act. In 1870, they opened a school, *Mikveh Yisrael*, not far from Jaffa and it continues to educate for this purpose to this day. Rabbi Kalisher's memory has been perpetuated in the name of a kibbutz, Tirat Zvi.

One of the most renowned rabbis of the nineteenth century was Rabbi Shmuel Mohlever (1824-1898) who served various communities until he settled in Bialystok in 1883. Not only was he exceptionally brilliant ad exceptionally learned (he was ordained at the age of 18), but he was also exceptionally active. His teachings became the basis of the later Mizrahi organization, a party of Orthodox Zionists who insisted upon the interrelationship of Jewish religion and modern nationalism.

Mohlever was so convinced of the need to engage in practical work to build a Jewish Palestine that he did not hesitate to join with secular Jews in creating the movement of *Hibbat Zion*. In the late 1870's, there were many study circles and fund-raising groups concerned about settling Jews in *Eretz Yisrael,* several having been initiated by Rabbi Mohlever, but they were not coordinated or organized into an overall movement. In 1884, a conference was called of all who were interested and those who attended formed the *Hibbat Zion* movement. Many Orthodox Jews refused to have anything to do with it because it included free-thinkers and secularists. Rabbi Shmuel Mohlever however, joined hands with all involved in settling in the Holy Land. Likewise, he accepted Herzl and the Zionist movement. He was absent from the first Zionist Congress because of poor health.

When Rabbi Mohlever travelled to the West to win the support of the Jewish notables, his greatest success was with Baron Edmond de Rothschild. Even if, as the Baron subsequently confided, he had already been concerned before his meeting with Mohlever, it was only after that meeting that he began to become directly involved and write checks for the would-be colonists. The first group for whom Mohilever elicited Rothschild's support established the colony of Ekron (or Mazkeret Batya).

On one of his many trips, Rabbi Mohlever met with Baron Ginzberg, the Russian Jewish mogul, who posed this question: "Let's say that you do set up a Jewish state in *Eretz Yisrael*. What will you do on *Shabbat* with the railroads, electricity, the telephone and the like?" The rabbi unhesitatingly replied: "First, *you* build a railroad and bring the telephone and electricity in *Eretz Yisrael*. Then with all the modern inventions that will be there, let us rabbis do research and I am certain that we will find a way to unite the Torah with the State."

In 1890, Rabbi Mohlever visited the Holy Land. After the trip he wrote:

Every parcel of land that is bought is fulfillment of the command to inherit the land, one of the most important *mitzvot* in the Torah..... True, we do not completely fulfill the *mitzvah* just by buying the land because the *mitzvah* has two parts: "You shall inherit the land and dwell therein". Purchase is partial fulfillment but the "dwelling" has not yet been carried out. The dwelling, according to the Ramban, is of two kinds: 1) living in the land and 2) settling it, i.e. we should live in it and also make it pleasant by planting and seeding.

My dear and cherished brothers who already have the privilege of going to the Holy Land and buying a piece of it, and who have also planted vineyards and built houses — you are fortunate. You will see your world in your lives. You are free from the ups and downs of business to which you had been chained, free from cheating and deception. Now you dwell in safety. You enjoy the fruit of your toil. You work the holy soil in serenity, without the tumult and uncertainties of business. You are so fortunate in the present and in the future! May God make our lot like yours. Amen.

(The Zionist Idea, p. 402)

In 1898, in honor of Rabbi Mohlever's 70th birthday, a grove of *etrog* trees were planted near Hadera. The place was named Gan Shmuel.

In every generation there have been great spiritual personalities and phenomenal scholars but every once in a while, there is one who is a level above them all. Such is Rabbi Avraham Hacohen Kook (1865-1935), an almost legendary figure, deeply beloved and revered. Even as a youth, his learning astounded everyone but so did his spirituality, his fervor in prayer, his sense of immediacy of God. Rabbi Kook firmly believed that the expression of modern Jewish nationalism was the beginning of an age in which the Messiah would appear, that the labors of the secularists must be lovingly accepted for they were unwittingly serving God's purposes.

Once, after he had become Chief Rabbi of Palestine, one of Rabbi Kook's pious followers asked him how he could befriend the irreligious pioneers. "The Torah tells us to love your neighbors as yourselves," the man continued. "I interpret the word *kamokha,* as yourself,' to mean one who is like you — pious, and scholarly. But if he scorns religion and does not practice it, you are not obligated to love him." Rabbi Kook replied: "I cannot accept your interpretation to love my neighbor only if he is like me. The true meaning is: "Love your neighbor as yourself". But if I love someone who is *not* like myself, then my love is *ahavat hinam,* a love without reservation, without cause. The Temple, we are told was destroyed because of *sinat hinam,* causeless hatred. Due to *sinat hinam* we were exiled. However, with *ahavat hinam* we may be worthy of redemption. For this reason we should love the *halutzim,* and all the people, even though they do not share our views. Only when we come to love our neighbor without reservation shall we bring about the redemption of Israel and all mankind."

In 1904, Rabbi Kook left Lithuania to become Chief Rabbi of Jaffa. Here, he had an exalted and ineffable religious experience which became the basis of his world-view. He wrote to a society of scholars in Jerusalem:

> The difference between the Torah of *Eretz Yisrael* and that of other lands is mighty and powerful. In *Eretz Yisrael*, the flow of the Holy Spirit bursts forth, ready to invade the minds of the scholars who seek to learn Torah for its own sake.
> ....But, the kind of sweetness and light of holiness that is offered in *Eretz Yisrael* to the scholars who seek God, is not found at all in other lands. And I can testify to this act out of my own experience.
>
> *(Banner of Jerusalem,* Agus, p. 69)

Rabbi Kook was out of the country during the years of World War I but returned in 1919 as Chief Rabbi of Jerusalem. Then, when the British established a chief rabbinate for all Jews of Palestine in 1921, Rabbi Kook held that post for the rest of his life.

Kook was a mystic who believed that all elements of the universe — the secular and the sacred, the human and the Divine, the physical and the spiritual — had to be united. That harmony did not exist because of *galut* (exile). But healing would come through the restoration of *Eretz Yisrael*.

> The realization that we are an awesome people, of royal descent, the nobles of the nations, can only be achieved on the soil of the Holy Land under the influence of the luminosity of the soul and the radiance of life.

Therefore, true Torah is only in *Eretz Yisrael* since the latter acts as a catalyst for the former.

(Orot Hatorah Chapter 13)

Rabbi Kook was unhappy with the division between the sacred and the secular in Zionism and pointed out that it was a grievous error. However, it was one he expected to be corrected.

The sacred must return to its status in our national Zionist movement, for only with it is the source of life. And then, too, it will revive through its strength, the secular values which were prepared and will be prepared to be of support. And this will be the path of repentance which will cure us from our sickness and will bring closer to complete redemption speedily and in our day...

(The Zionist Idea, p. 419)

Kook maintained that the spirit of God was the road of the national spirit, even when not recognized. Therefore, it was not permissible to oppose Jewish nationalism. Those who did recognize the spirit of God must "work all the harder at the task of uncovering the light and holiness implicit in our national spirit, the divine element which is at its core. The secularists will be constrained to realize that they are immersed and rooted in the life of God and bathed in the radiant sanctity that comes from above."

(ibid.)

Rabbi Kook taught that the Return to Zion, the agriculture and industry and rebuilding was more than met the eye. He saw in it a secret goal, that of *tikkun olam*, improving this world into a kingdom of God.

A well-to-do Jew from Denver visited the Holy Land and called upon the Chief Rabbi. He complained about the lack of piety he saw, especially the lack of religion on the part of the *halutzim*. Rabbi Kook responded by asking his visitor about Denver. The American bragged about the climate and the fine hospitals. With seeming naivete, the rabbi said: " I heard that Denver was filled with tuberculars. Doesn't that mean it is an unhealthy city?" The visitor responded: "On the contrary. Because of the wonderful climate, tuberculosis hospitals have been established and sick people from all over come to live here. Thereupon Rabbi Kook said: "Even so, sick Jewish souls from all parts of the world come to sink their roots in the Holy Land, there to be renewed and reinvigorated."

In the early decades of the nineteenth century, Karl Marx formulated his theories and won over many adherents who were eager to create a better, indeed an ideal, world. Several young Jews who had left their homes and tradition thought that socialism was the answer to the problems of civilization. One such person was Moses Hess (1812-1875). He came from an observant home and received a good Jewish education but left it all after a quarrel with his father. He became a friend of Marx and believed that the salvation of mankind lay in the universal adoption of socialism. At the same time, Hess did not completely abandon his Jewish ties and he retained concern for his people. Indeed, one of his circle dubbed him "the communist rabbi"!

Hess began to question his new ideas and new

companions after "the Damascus Affair" of 1840. This was a world scandal. The Jews of Damascus were accused of murdering a priest in order to use his blood for religious purposes. The ensuing suffering and torture aroused Montefiore and others to intervene and alleviate the situation. Hess later attributed his return to his people to the Damascus Affair.

> Then it dawned on me for the first time in the midst of my socialistic activities that I belong to my unfortunate, slandered, despised and dispersed people.

He did not thereupon · give up his socialistic concerns, even when he was faced with personal anti-Semitic experiences. But he continued to reflect upon his people, particularly after the Italian struggle for unity and independence met with success. Moreover, Rabbi Kalisher's writings had a deep effect on him. It was only until 1861 that he published his book which won him his place in history: *Rome and Jerusalem*. This work presented a candid and bold description of Western Jewry together with a diagnosis of its ills and a program for the future.

Hess wrote *Rome and Jerusalem*, in the form of twelve letters, an epilogue and ten Supplementary Notes. He often digressed but he made his points clearly. The book opened with an amazing personal confession:

> After an estrangement of twenty years, I am back with my people. I have come to be one of them again, to participate in the celebration of the holy days, to share the memories and hopes of the nation, to take

part in the spiritual and intellectual warfare going on within the House of Israel...
A thought which I believed to be forever buried in my heart has been revived in me anew. It is the thought of my nationality, which is inseparably connected with the ancestral heritage and the memories of the Holy Land, the Eternal City, the birthplace of the belief in the divine unity of life, as well as the hope in the future brotherhood of men. (First Letter).

Hess unequivocally asserted that the Jews were a nation. Just as all nations were rooted in a land, so were the Jews.

Among the nations believed to be dead, and which, when they become conscious of their historic mission, will struggle for their national rights, is also Israel — the nation which for two thousand years has defied the storms of time, and in spite of having been tossed by the currents of history to every part of the globe, has always cast yearning glances toward Jerusalem and is still directing its gaze thither.

Fortified by its racial instinct and by its cultural and historical mission to unite all humanity in the name of the Eternal Creator, this people has conserved its nationality, in the form of its religion, and united both inseparably with the memories of its ancestral land. No modern people, struggling for its own fatherland, can deny the right of the Jewish people to its former land, without at the same time undermining the justice of its own strivings.

(Preface)

Hess called for a political organization to enable Jews to return to Palestine and reconstitute themselves as a nation. He saw the root of the Jewish problem as homelessness and its solution a Jewish state. He called for a congress of the Great Powers to create a Jewish Palestine convinced that it would benefit non-Jews as well as Jews.

The growing rather than the lessening of anti-Semitism as the nineteenth century progressed disillusioned many of those Jews who had thought that the improvement of the Jewish lot would come as Jews became less Jewish and more like their hosts. One such personality was Dr. Leon Pinsker (1821-1891), a Russian Jew whose scholarly father failed to give his son a deep Jewish education. Pinsker went to law school at the University of Moscow and then to medical school, choosing to practice in Odessa. He and his friends were convinced that they should devote themselves to the liberalization of all Russia rather than limit themselves to the "narrow" Jewish problem. They did not leave the Jewish community but expended their energies in urging Jews to become like the majority.

Pinsker began having doubts about these goals after a pogrom in 1871, when the Russian intellectuals not only failed to condemn the perpetrators but actually joined them. After the pogroms of 1881, he realized that assimilation was utter folly ad soon wrote down his analyses of the Jewish problem and suggested a cure. He wrote a pamphlet entitled "Autoemancipation", adopting for its heading the famous saying of Hillel (the great 1st century rabbi): "If I am not for myself, who will be for me?"

This is the kernel of the problem, as we see it: The Jews comprise a distinctive element among the nations under which they dwell, and as such can neither assimilate nor be readily digested by any nation.

Hence the solution lies in finding a means of so readjusting this exclusive element to the family of nations, that the basis of the Jewish question will be permanently removed.

("Auto-Emancipation",
ZOA Pamphlet, p. 7)

Pinsker diagnosed anti-Semitism as a disease, a psychic aberration that could not be removed by reasoning. He called this disease "Judeophobia".

Pinsker maintained that the disease was so deeply imbedded that nothing could change it. Jews may try their best to be accepted but they would never be at home. "Since the Jew is nowhere at home, nowhere regarded as a native, he remains an alien everywhere. That he himself and his ancestors as well are born in the country does not alter this fact in the least." Therefore, Jews should seek their own salvation and to do what they needed for a home of their own.

We must seek our honor and our salvation not in self-deception but in the restoration of our national ties. Hitherto the world has not considered us a firm of standing, and consequently we enjoy no genuine credit.

If other national movements which have risen before our eyes their own justification, can it still be questioned whether the Jews have a similar right? They play a larger part in the life of the civilized nations, and they have rendered a greater service to humanity; they have a greater past and history, a common, unmixed descent, an indestructible vigor, an unshakable faith and an unexampled martyrology; the peoples have sinned against them more grievously than against any other nation. Is not that enough to make them capable and worthy of possessing a fatherland?

(pp. 18-19)

Pinsker suggested the convocation of a congress to buy a territory for the settlement of several million Jews. It was only after he published his pamphlet that he recognized that *Eretz Yisrael* alone could be that territory. However, even as one who would accept any territory at all, he knew the need for immediate action and concluded "Autoemancipation":

Let "Now or never" be our watchword. Woe to our descendants, woe to the memory of our Jewish contemporaries, if we let this moment pass by! Help yourself and God will help you!

(p. 28)

Dr. Pinsker at no time expected to be a leader or become involved in organizational matters but he did agree to head the *Hibbat Zion* movement, because he felt it was his duty. However, he was neither a politician nor an administrator nor could he cope with the conflict between the Orthodox and the Secularists. Accordingly, he resigned after two years but continued to be revered, honored for calling his people to free themselves.

One of the most influential Hebrew writers of his era was Peretz Smolenskin (1842-1885) who, after many years of wandering, settled in Vienna where he founded a journal he named *Hashakhar*. This paper quickly became the leading one of the 1870s and marked the beginning of a new age in Hebrew literature, that of national awakening. In several essays and novels, Smolenskin emphasized that assimilation was not possible nor would it bring personal happiness. Even though Jews lacked a geographical basis, they were nevertheless a nation — a "Spiritual" nation.

The Jewish People has outlived all the others because it has always regarded itself as a people — a spiritual nation. Without exception its sages and writers, its prophets and the authors of its prayers, have always called it a people. Clearly, therefore, this one term has sufficient power to unite those who are dispersed all over the world. Jews of different countries regard and love one another as members of the same people because they remember that the tie that binds them did not begin yesterday; it is four thousand years old.....

(The Zionist Idea, p. 145)

Later, after 1881, Smolenskin became more aware of the need for *Eretz Yisrael* and became a follower of *Hibbat Zion*.

A policy of reducing the number of Jews in the countries where they are hated can be successful only if substantial segments of the Jewish communities emigrate.... There is no doubt that it would be best for people who are leaving one country to migrate together to the same new land, for they could then understand and help one another. If the wave of emigration is to direct itself to one place, surely no other country in the world is conceivable except *Eretz Yisrael*.

(ibid, p. 151)

Smolenskin held that it was impossible to persuade Jews who hate Zion or those who refused to budge until the Messiah arrived. For others, he listed six benefits which *Eretz Yisrael* had over other countries:

1. Those who cherish the memory of their ancestors will gladly go there, if they can be assured that they will make a living.

2. The country is not too distant from their former homes.

3. All the emigrants could live together in the manner of their accustomed traditions.

4. Those who now live in idleness in the Land of Israel will gradually acquire a new spirit, which will lead them to a life of productive labor. Thousands will therefore be saved from all the evils which such idleness creates.

5. Not everyone will have to work on the land for if some turn to agriculture, the others can successfully devote themselves to commerce....

6. Settlers could prosper by establishing factories for glass and allied products for the sand of the country is of high quality.

(ibid, p. 153)

Even in his last days, alone and sick, Smolenskin wrote enthusiastically about the Return to Zion. Just a few days before he died, he completed his long novel *Hayerusha*, The Inheritance.

Hibbat Zion was just the right answer to the searching of Moshe Leib Lilienblum (1843-1910) who grew up studying Talmud intensively and, as a young man, finding such dissatisfaction with the religion he knew that he left home. The unhappy, dour Lilienblum settled in Odessa, the great city, which became the center of Jewish Enlightenment. He soon became disillusioned with finding it spiritually empty and leading to vulgar, assimilation. Now that he had lost religious faith, he had nothing in its place. He turned to literature and wrote his autobiography *(Hatat Neurim-Sins of My Youth)* which has been called "one of the saddest books any Jew ever wrote"

The pogroms of 1881 had a shocking effect on him. Realizing that, even where they were not persecuted, Jews everywhere were at best merely tolerated, Lilienblum realized that they had a home somewhere — and that could be only *Eretz Yisrael.*

> We must undertake the colonization of Palestine on so comprehensive a scale that, in the course of one century, the Jews may be able to leave inhospitable Europe almost entirely and settle in the land of our forefathers, to which we are legally entitled.

Here was a course of action for all Jews, for the Jewish nation. The Jews were a nation; their religion was a national religion. In his essay *Derek Tesuvah* (Way of Return), written in 1881 he said:

Yes, we are strangers. We are not only strangers here, but in all Europe, for it is not the birthplace of our people. What is our future? Terrible, very terrible: there is no spark of hope, no ray of light, slaves, aliens and strangers we shall be eternally exposed to mockery and shame! But, the land of our fathers? Why should we be aliens in strange lands at the time when the land of our fathers is not yet erased from the globe and is capable, in combination with its neighboring territories, to produce room for our people?

In an essay written the following year, Lilienblum asserted that the unity of the Jewish people depended in their return, that in Palestine individuals could differ as much as they pleased:

The nation as a whole is dearer to all of us than all the divisions over rigid Orthodoxy or liberalism in religious observances put together. Where the nation is concerned there are no sects or denominations, there are neither modern nor old-fashioned men, no devout or heretics, but all are Children of Abraham, Isaac and Jacob! There is no logic in any desire for all the future Jewish settlers in the ancestral land to belong to the exact same sect. Let each man there follow the dictates of his conscience; let the Hasidim there put on two sets of *tephilin*, and let the more liberal recite the Shema and say the prayers where they will without *tephilin*, let the Orthodox send their children to the *hadarim* of Lithuania and

Poland, and let the Maskilim (Enlightened) set up schools patterned after the secular schools in Europe. But let no man oppress his fellow. Within our autonomous political life everything will find its place. Unite and join forces; let us gather our dispersed from Eastern Europe and go up to our land with rejoicing; whoever is on the side of God and His People, let him say: I am for Zion. To be sure, it is a great complicated task, but is a nation born all at once? We must work for the development of our land, and we have no right to shirk this divine task.

Lilienblum was fully aware that colonization was a long process involving countless details but that made no difference. That was the task to be done. Lilienblum never became involved in Herzl's Zionist Organization because he paid no attention to diplomacy or politics. Nor did he care much about cultural matters. He was one of the founders of *Hibbat Zion*. He worked intimately with Pinsker and served as the movement's secretary. His sole concern was colonization and its needs. He ignored those who made fun of his Zionism of "one more goat and one more colony", persisting in tending to settlement matters and the needs of the settlers the rest of his life.

Discussion Questions

1) How do the views expressed by these rabbis (especially Kook) concerning studying Torah in Israel relate to the sayings of the Rabbis found in chapter II?

2) Rabbi Kook expressed his love for all Jews, no matter their level of commitment. The Gaon of Vilna, as we saw in chapter IV, decided not to go to Israel because he thought he would feel religiously uncomfortable. How do you think you would feel living as a Conservative Jew in Orthodox run Israel? Should there be religious pluralism in Israel? To what extent? (See the last chapter) How would Lilienblum respond?

3) We have seen from Rabbi Kalisher and others, the view that if Jews settle in Israel that would hasten the coming of the Messiah. Yet there are still many ultra-Orthodox Jews today who believe that the state of Israel should not exist *until* the Messiah comes. Do you agree with the ultra-Orthodox or with Rabbi Kalisher? Why?

4) Would any of the six benefits listed by Smolenskin for living in *Eretz Yisrael*, convince you to live in Israel?

5) It seems that the major impetus for establishing a Jewish homeland was European anti-Semitism. Had it not been for anti-Semitism, do you think the state of Israel would have been established in 1948? Since you live in a land which, from its inception, has been relatively free from anti-Semitism, can you empathize with Pinsker et. al.?

Chapter 7

A. POLITICAL ZIONISM

Zionism as a movement, as more than an emotional expression of love for *Eretz Yisrael* and support of brave Jews who dared to settle in the ancestral homeland, as an organization aiming to establish a state for Jews in Palestine, was the creation of Theodor Herzl (1860-1904).

When one looks back on Herzl's life and career before he conceived the idea of a Jewish state, one would never have expected him to emerge as one of the major personalities of Jewish history. Herzl was born in Budapest to parents who were not very concerned about Jewish matters. He routinely became a Bar Mitzvah but otherwise had little to do with the synagogue or Jewish Life. There were confrontations with some anti-Semitism in his life but they did not prevent him from becoming a very successful journalist and playwright. Posted in Paris, he sent back to his paper in Vienna delightful columns that won him a highly acclaimed reputation.

While in Paris, Herzl witnessed the unfolding of the Dreyfus Affair. Captain Alfred Dreyfus, a Frenchman and officer in the French army was framed by another French officer. Dreyfus was accused of spying for the Germans and thus was brought to trial for treason. He was accused and sent to the prison camp on Devil's Island. The case dragged on for years and finally Dreyfus was acquitted of all charges. But over the course of this whole affair anti-Semitism became rampant in France. The Dreyfus affair radically changed Herzl. The testimonies offered in court made him recognize that the accusations and verdict against Captain Alfred Dreyfus were fabrications, evidence of blatant anti-Semitism. He looked about him and became aware of the depth of Jew-hatred anywhere. As he thought of the Jewish problem more and more, he decided to express his thoughts in writing.

In 1896, he published the *Der Judenstaadt, The Jewish State*, the now-famous booklet, written with masterful clarity and great certainty. In the preface, Herzl stated:

> The idea which I have developed in this pamphlet is a very old one: the restoration of Jewish State.
> The earth resounds with outcries against the Jews, and these outcries have awakened the slumbering idea..... .
> I am absolutely convinced that I am right — though, I doubt whether I shall live to see myself proved to be so. Those who are the first to inaugurate this movement will scarcely live to see its glorious close. But the inauguration of it is enough to give them self-respect and the joy of freedom of the soul!
>
> (Jacob de Haas translation of
> *A Jewish State*)

Herzl asserted that the Jews were considered an alien body everywhere and it was futile to argue that they were not. Rather than wait for some Utopian solution, it was better to act, to gather all Jews to a land of their own and thereby give birth to a new freedom.

No human being is wealthy or powerful enough to transplant a nation from one habitation to another. An idea alone can encompass that: and this idea of a State may have the requisite power to do so. The Jews have dreamt this kingly dream all through the long nights of their history. "Next Year in Jerusalem" is our old phrase. It is now a question of showing that the dream can be converted into a living reality.

(ibid.)

Herzl knew enough and felt deeply enough about Judaism to set the expected Jewish State in Palestine and not simply in any territory available. Indeed, he envisioned such a state as a boon for both Islam and Christianity. Herzl not only argued the case for a Jewish state but dealt with practicalities as well. He proposed the creation of two agencies: "The Society of Jews" and "The Jewish Company". One would organize the masses, educate public opinion and deal with the Great Powers. The other would be responsible for raising funds to move Jews and supervise the economic rebuilding of the State.

Herzl decided to convoke an assembly of all sympathetic to his ideas. Before the Congress opened on August 19, 1897, Herzl wrote in his diary: "The fact is... that I have only an army of *schnorrers*. I am

in command only of boys, beggars, and prigs."
After the Congress, however, he recorded:

I do not know how much fate will still
permit me to see of the realization of our
idea, whether I will be present when the
Jewish people begins to make the land of
our fathers fruitful and flourishing, to build
streets, harbors, railroads, canals,
waterworks, houses, fine cities and the
temple. But this I do know, that on that
August Sunday of 1897, in Basle, I
experienced the whole movement has to
give. On that day,the Jewish people found
itself once more. Two hundred representatives of organizations from all over the
world gathered together in Basle, I
experienced something tremendous, perhaps
the greatest thing that the whole movement
has to give. On that day the Jewish people
found itself once more. Two hundred
representatives of organizations from all
over the world gathered together in Basle,
and they declared amidst Jewish people, that
this people has not succumbed and does not
want to succumb. That is the main thing.
When once a people's consciousness and a
people's will are in evidence then all that
remains is to find sensible ways and means
to realize them. A people is inexhaustible in
strength just as it is not limited by the time
limits of an individual. Naturally, the
realization ought not be unduly delayed, or
else the clearest strivings grow pale and
unreal as dreams... Accordingly, we did not
tarry overmuch among the sentimental

dreams of rediscovery but made every effort to go forward.

In his opening address to that first Congress, Dr. Herzl declared: "Zionism is the return of the Jews to Judaism, even before their return to the Jewish land." He was elected President and immediately devoted his entire life, body and soul to further the Zionist goal. On May 2, 1902, he wrote in his diary: "Today I am 41 years old.....It is nearly six years since I began this movement which has made me old, tired and poor." Yet, despite critics from within and lack of success in attaining commitments from the Great Powers, Herzl wrote, shortly after the Fifth Congress:

Zionism is the Sabbath of my life. I think that my success as a leader is due to the fact that I, who as a man and an author have so many weaknesses, have made so many mistakes, and have committed so many foolish acts, was completely unselfish in the Zionist cause.

In October of 1902, Herzl published a novel entitled *Alteneuland* (Old-New Land. Nahum Sokolow translated it into Hebrew and called it *Tel Aviv*.) It was a story of the Jewish Palestine he envisaged. It portrayed cities and farms, equality and men and women, free education, Arab and Jews as friends and tolerance for all. The motto which Herzl chose for his novel was: "If you will it, it is no legend" אִם תִּרְצוּ אֵין זוֹ אַגָּדָה.

Herzl worked to the point of exhaustion, ignoring his serious cardiac problems, and died at 44, on July 3, 1904. The entire Jewish world went into mourning. Ahad Ha'am, one of his severe critics, wrote: "One thing is beyond all doubt: to form such a movement..... could have been done only by a man who had in him a rare spark of genius, a man like those who arrive from time to time among every people and conquer the desired path". At the first Zionist Congress a flag was adopted as well as a national hymn (Hatikvah). And the official program of the Zionist movement, known ever since as *The Basle Program*. It is the first basic document of the Zionist movement. It stated: "Zionism seeks to secure for the Jewish people a publicly recognized legally secured home (or homeland) in Palestine for Jewish people". For the achievement of its purpose the Congress envisaged the following methods:

1. The programmatic encouragement of the settlement of Palestine with Jewish agricultural workers, laborers and artisans;

2. The unification and organization of all Jewry into local and general groups in accordance with the laws for their respective countries;

3. The strengthening of Jewish self-awareness and national consciousness;

4. The preparation of activity for the obtaining of the consent of the various governments, necessary for the fulfillment of the aim of Zionism.

(*Theodore Herzl*, Bein p. 239)

When Theodore Herzl first formulated his idea, he showed a friend what he had written. The friends became worried abut Herzl's mental and emotional state and suggested that he go to the renowned Dr. Max Nordau (1849-1923). The story goes that Nordau said to Herzl: "If you are crazy, so am I!" and thereupon became one of Herzl's most ardent supporters. At the time that he espoused *The Jewish State* few people even knew that the internationally noted writer, scholar and critic was a Jew.

Nordau was the son of an Orthodox rabbi in Budapest. As a teen-ager, he earned his living by his pen and left his Judaism behind while pursuing higher education. A gifted linguist and possessor of a brilliant mind, he travelled and wrote novels, journalistic pieces and philosophical and sociological works. Living in Paris, Nordau attacked the decadent culture of his day and charged that it threatened the future of civilization. He warned against excessive nationalism but regarded healthy nationalism as valuable. After the Dreyfus Affair, Nordau became painfully aware of the deep-rootedness of anti-Semitism and was thus ready for what Theodor Herzl had to propose.

When the Congress met in 1897, Max Nordau gave the main address, as he did at nine subsequent congresses. The American rabbi, Stephen S. Wise, once commented that he had "heard the great tribunes of the East and of the West, but I have never heard a human speak as Nordau spoke in the early days of the Zionist congresses. The burden of prophecy was laid upon him."

The motive for Nordau's Zionism was not the Bible or the prayerbook. He accepted Herzl's plan because he had come to realize how desperately the Jews needed a home.

Why have we become Zionists? Because of a mystic desire for Zion? We have become Zionists because the distress of the Jewish race has appealed to our hearts, because we see with sorrow a steadily increasing misery which will lead to sudden and calamitous catastrophes, and because our earnest and painful investigations show us but one way out of the labyrinth of affliction, and that is the acquisition of a legally assured and guaranteed home for the persecuted Jewish millions. How different the position would be today if we could say to our Roumanian brethren: "Come, here is the country which is awaiting you, as a mother does her returning sons."

(Max Nordau to His People, Scopus Pub.Co. p. 117)

Between Congresses Nordau addressed many groups, seeking to infuse them with pride and the will-to-liberation. With brilliance and logic he would analyze the causes of anti-Semitism and expose the sham of assimilation. When Herzl dies, Nordau was urged to assume leadership of the movement but he refused. He was not prepared to devote himself exclusively to Zionism activities. Nevertheless, he was always regarded as the real leader. Everyone was deeply moved when, in the course of his address to the Ninth Congress (in 1909), he declared:

My ideal is to see a Jewish people in the land of its fathers, ennobled by a two-thousand-year-old firmness of character, respected on account of its honest and fruitful cultural work, an instrument of wise progress, a champion of justice, an apostle and personifier of brotherly love. Of this idea I will not surrender an iota. On this point there can be no concession. This ideal I would not exchange for all the treasure in the world, let alone for a dividend. If Turkey today opposes the realization of my ideal, I must wait long, wait in pain. To wait long is a misfortune, but it is no disgrace. Vacillation is a disgrace. My ideal is eternal. It embraces every hope. To abandon hope, however, is to commit suicide.

(p. 188)

When the World Zionist Organization came into being, it was an undivided body. Soon, however, groups within it formed to seek their specific kind of Zionism. The Orthodox, for example, formed Mizrachi, a party seeking a Zionism adhering to Orthodox Judaism. Those who believed in a combination of Socialism and Zionism created their own parties,. Their were those who were "General Zionists," without a specific ideology but not committed to any other. And then there was another, not established until the twenties — the Revisionists, whose founder and leader was Vladimir Jabotinsky (1880-1940).

Jabotinsky was a man of rare gifts, one who possessed exceptional talents and a stormy personality. He inspired deep admiration on the one hand and intense hostility on the other. He was a magnificent orator, a brilliant writer, a remarkable linguist, a fine soldier and a keen statesman. But he was also erratic, obstinate, severely critical and ultimately unwilling to be bound by the discipline of a movement.

Jabotinsky was born in Odessa, a large city that became the center of the Jewish Enlightenment, not noted for Jewish piety and learning. The intelligent young man was rather indifferent to matters Jewish and turned to his people only after the threat of a pogrom brought him to realize the validity of Zionism. He became active locally, attended the sixth Zionist Congress and never forgot the impact of Herzl. He wrote in his autobiography:

Herzl made a colossal impression on me — the word is no empty phrase. There is no other description that will fit — but colossal — and I am not easily impressed by personalities. Of all my acquaintances I remember no person who made such an impression on me, not anyone before Herzl, nor anyone after him. Here I felt that I really stood before a man chosen by fate, before a prophet and leader — that even to err and blunder in following him was justified. And to this day it seems that we still hear the resounding voice as he swore efore us: "If I forget thee, Jerusalem," I believed his pledge. Everyone believed.

He threw himself into Zionist work, demanding that it become more activist and more militant. He came to hate the *galut* (Diaspora) and wanted his fellow-Jews to throw off its spirit of submission and inferiority; he longed for a Jewish life that would be proud, bold and aggressive.

During World War I Jabotinsky urged the formation of a Jewish military unit to fight with the Allies for the liberation of Palestine and was instrumental in creating the Jewish Legion for that purpose. After the War, when a Zionist Commission was appointed to examine the country's needs and plan for the future, he was appointed a member by Chaim Weizmann. But Weizmann soon had reason to regret his appointment for, though he recognized Jabotinsky's great intelligence, he was continually irked by him. Jabotinsky was constantly protesting the slowness of attaining statehood, the seeming giving-in to the British.

Living in Jerusalem after the War, Jabotinsky became the leader of the newly organized *Haganah* (Defence Force), directing his men in defense action against rioters. The British arrested him and sentenced him to fifteen years in jail. He was subsequently freed but always regarded with suspicion. At the end of the decade, Jabotinsky was denied permission to live in Palestine.

During the twenties, Jabotinsky decided that his place was still within the World Zionist Organization, that he could persuade his colleagues to take stronger stands against the British and to increase immigration substantially.

Jabotinsky was so opposed to Weizmann's policy of compromise that he could no longer remain on the Executive and resigned in 1923. When he left, he intended to withdraw from politics altogether for a time but he was just not able to do so. He soon decided to form his own party, Revisionism, as the true heir of Herzl and Nordau. They would no longer make concession after concession but would press hard for "the gradual transformation of Palestine (including Transjordan) into a self-governing commonwealth under the auspices of an established Jewish majority."

As time went on, Jabotinsky's opposition to socialism estranged him all the more from the Labor parties and his adherents often clashed with their antagonists. Increasingly, he felt that he had no place in the World Zionist Organization. In 1935, he concluded that he must leave and he proceeded to organize his own: "The New Zionist Organization." Its aim was to create a Jewish state on both sides of the Jordan and to gather in all Jews. It organized its own military forces, the Irgun, with Jabotinsky as supreme commander.

When Jabotinsky appeared before the Palestine Royal Commission which met in the House of Lords in early 1937, he came as a representative of The New Zionist Organization and made it clear that it differed in many respects from the World Zionist Organization. It would not compromise on the issue of statehood. In his testimony, he declared:

> When I pronounce the words "a Jewish State" I think of a Jewish State" I think of a commonwealth, or an area, enjoying a certain sufficient amount of self-government in its internal and external affairs, and possessing a Jewish majority.... The term "Palestine" when I employ it will mean the areas on both sides of the Jordan, the area mentioned in the original Palestine Mandate.

Jabotinsky continued by asserting that Palestine could hold from eight to eighteen million inhabitants and went on to make clear why a Jewish state was an absolute necessity.

> We are facing an elemental calamity, a kind of social earthquake. ...the cause of our suffering is the very fact of the Diaspora,

the bedrock fact that we are everywhere a minority. It is not the anti-Semitism of things, the inherent xenophobia of the body social or the body economic under which we suffer. Of course, there are ups and downs; but moments, there are whole periods in history when this "xenophobia of Life Itself" takes dimensions which no people can stand and that is what we are facing now. ...it is humanity's duty to provide the Jews with an area where they could build up their own body social undisturbed by anyone.

(An Answer to Ernest Bevin)

Jabotinsky never lost hope nor allowed others to lose hope. When a young man wrote to him to express his disillusionment and despair, Jabotinsky replied:

Your generation is destined to see miracles, and collectively perform miracles. Don't get downhearted because of the butcheries going on: everything, all forces of life and death are now converging toward one end, Jewish State and great Exodus to Palestine.

I think, on a very conservative estimate, that the next ten years will see the Jewish State of Palestine not only proclaimed but a reality...

Mon ami, I should be thrilled every hour of my wake and dream, if I had the luck of being 20 today on the threshold of redeemed Israel and probably, a redeemed world to

boot; no matter what butcheries it may cost
(*The Jerusalem Post Weekly*, July 10, 1964)

The conflict between the Haganah, the defense force of the organized Jewish community of Palestine (i.e. subject to the World Zionist Organization) and the Irgun grew. It was impossible to achieve reconciliation or unification. In June of 1939, Jabotinsky drafted a "Call to Jewish Youth" which began with the statement: "We have come to the conclusion that the only way to liberate our country is by the sword." When World War II broke out, Jabotinsky tried to persuade the British Government to approve the formation of a Jewish army. Unable to enlist any sympathy, he went to the United States in 1940 to try to win American support. He was depressed, gloomy, and in poor health. While visiting the *Betar* camp in Hunter, New York in July, he had an angina attack and died. He was buried in the New Montefiore Cemetery on Long Island. Several years before, he had written a will in which he stipulated: "Should I die outside Palestine I want to be buried or cremated (it is the same to me) just wherever I happen to die; and my remains may *not* be transferred to Palestine unless by order of that country's eventual Jewish Government." It was not until 1964 that the State of Israel arranged for Jabotinsky's remains to be removed to Jerusalem.

All of the Zionist leaders were more or less deeply rooted in Jewish life and Jewish sources. Even Jabotinsky, who had not studied in a *heder* or *yeshiva*, became a master of the Hebrew language to such a degree that he translated Bialik and others. Louis Dembitz Brandies (1856-1941), however, knew nothing of Jewish observances or culture. Born in Louisville, Kentucky to parents who practiced little of the Jewish religion, he went to Harvard after completing high school. He graduated Law School and quickly became one of the country's finest lawyers. In 1916, President Wilson appointed Brandeis to the Supreme Court. He was already a prominent Zionist leader at that time but could not remain an official of the organization once he became a Justice.

Brandeis had never been an outright assimilationist nor had he ever renounced Judaism. However, he was not brought up to attend synagogue or to observe religious rituals. He gave charity to Jewish causes but he also did so to non-Jewish causes. In his long carer he was not confronted with any overt anti-Semitism nor been rebuffed for being a Jew. Yet he identified himself as one and came to regard his great concern for social justice as part of his Jewish heritage. This prepared the way for him to embrace Zionism.

In 1910, Brandies was asked to mediate a strike of the New York garment workers (mostly Jews) and was deeply impressed by the interest of working men and women in intellectual and social problems and by their sense of pride and self-worth despite degrading conditions. He was amazed to hear a pale worker lecturing his employer with a Hebrew quotation from Isaiah: "What mean ye that ye beat my people to pieces and grind the faces of the poor?"

Later that year, Jacob de Haas (once Herzl's English secretary) interviewed Brandeis and spent two hours telling him about Herzl and Zionism. Brandeis began reading up on the subject and, in 1912 joined the Federation of American Zionists. It was not long before he not only began to attend meetings but to chair them as well. After World War I broke out, the situation in Palestine became desperate, Brandeis agreed to serve as chairman of the Provisional

Executive Committee for General Zionist Affairs. He was not a mere figurehead; he became a true leader. He travelled, raised funds, wrote articles and gave addresses. In 1915 he published a pamphlet — "The Jewish Question" — in which he asserted:

Zionism seeks to establish in Palestine, for such Jews as choose to go and remain there, and for their descendants, a legally secured home, where they may live together and lead a Jewish life, where they may expect ultimately to constitute a majority of the population, and may look forward in what we should call home rule. The Zionists seek to establish this home in Palestine because they are convinced that the undying longing of Jews for Palestine is a fact of deepest significance...

Even though Brandies did not know Hebrew and was not fully appreciative of the cultural rebirth that was part of the birth of Zion he nevertheless understood the significance of the revival of the Hebrew language. "Perhaps the most extraordinary achievement of Jewish nationalism is the revival of the Hebrew language, which has again become a language of the common intercourse of men. The Hebrew tongue, called a dead language for nearly two thousand years, has in the Jewish colonies and in Jerusalem, become again the living mother tongue. The effect of this common language in unifying the Jews is, of course, great; for the Jews of Palestine came literally from all the lands of the earth, each speaking, except for the use of Yiddish, the language of the country from which he came, and remaining in the main, almost a stranger to the others. But the effect of the renaissance of the Hebrew tongue is far greater than that of unifying the Jews. It is a potent factor in reviving the essentially Jewish spirit.

Our Jewish Pilgrim Fathers have had the foundation. It remains for us to build the superstructure."

One of the most virulent charges against Zionism was that of dual loyalties. How could one be loyal to America and, at the same time, loyal to the cause of a Jewish state? The superpatriots held that the second was in conflict with the first. It was the Kentucky-bred Boston aristocrat who gave the resounding answers.

"Let no American imagine that Zionism is inconsistent with Patriotism. Multiple loyalties are objectionable only if they are inconsistent. A man is a better citizen of the United States for being loyal to his family, and to his profession or trade; for being loyal to his college or his lodge. Every Irish- American who contributed towards advancing home rule was a better man and a better American for the sacrifice he made. Every American Jew who aids in advancing the Jewish settlement in Palestine, though he feels that neither he nor his descendants will ever live there, will likewise be a better man and a better American for doing so. ...

There is no inconsistency between loyalty to America and loyalty to Jewry. The Jewish spirit, the product of our religion and experiences, is essentially modern and essentially American. Not since the destruction of the Temple have the Jews in spirit and in ideals been so fully in harmony with the noblest aspirations of the country in which they lived."

In a message to the Jewish Daily News of Boston in June of 1915, Brandeis called for a publicly recognized, legally secured home for the Jews in

Palestine but added that success could not come "unless the Jews organize effectively now to grasp the opportunity offered." And he repeated his faith in Zionists being good Americans.

Let the Loyal Jews stand up and be counted. Every Jew owes that duty to America as well as to Judaism. For to be a good American, he must be a good Jew. And to be a good Jew, he must be a Zionist.

During World War I Brandeis kept his friend President Wilson informed about the goals and aims of Zionism and was a principle influence in securing American backing for the Balfour Declaration. He was in constant communication with Weizmann and wrote the policy statement of the Zionist Organization of America, one which affirmed anew "the principles which were the foundation of the ancient Jewish state and of the living Jewish law embodied in the traditions of 2,000 years of exile."

In the years following World War I, Brandeis differed sharply with Weizmann. He believed that the political struggle of Zionism had ended with Great Britain receiving the Mandate. To him, the task of the Zionist Organization henceforward was raising funds to invest wisely in Palestine. The struggle was not over major principles but over specific organizational reforms. Weizmann knew that the political achievements had to be guarded well and was not prepared to give up the political and cultural responsibilities of the Zionist Organization. He believed that the fight for Jewish sovereignty had to be continued.

Chaim Weizmann (1874-1953) was one of the few early Zionist leaders who lived to celebrate the birth of the State of Israel. He was dedicated to the cause of the Jewish people returning to *Eretz Yisrael* even when he was a young child. When only eleven years old, he was sent to school from his hometown Motel to nearby Pinsk. Weizmann wrote to his teacher back home:

How lofty and elevated the idea which inspired our brothers, the Sons of Israel, to establish the Hovevei Society. Because of this we can rescue our exiled, oppressed brethren who are scattered in all corners of the world and have no place where to put up their tents...Let us carry our banner to Zion and return to our first mother upon whose knees we were born.
...In conclusion, to Zion! — Jews — to Zion! let us go.

(The Letters and Papers of Chaim Weizmann, vol.1, pp.36-37)

As a student majoring in biochemistry at the University of Berlin, Weizmann found time to participate in an organization of fellow Russian Zionists which preached Jewish nationalism. He responded to Herzl however with caution. He believed that Zionism had to include cultural work and practical projects in *Eretz Yisrael* in addition to diplomatic efforts to attain a state. He joined together with like-minded young people to form an opposition group to Herzl. After teaching and doing scientific work in Geneva for a few years, Weizmann moved to the University of Manchester in Manchester, England. At first, he kept aloof from active Zionist involvement but he could not do so for long. He soon met Arthur

James Balfour to whom he explained the Jews attachment to Palestine.

In 1914, when Balfour was First Lord of the Admirality, a colleague arranged an interview for Weizmann with him. He sent a note to introduce Weizmann and Balfour wrote back: "Weizmann needs no introduction. I still remember our conversation in 1906." When Weizmann came to his office, Balfour greeted him with: "Well, you haven't changed much since we met. You know I was thinking of that conversation of ours, and I believe that when the guns stop firing you may get your Jerusalem."

During the World War I years, Weizmann not only headed Zionist work but also developed a special process for producing acetone, a substance Britain needed in making explosives for naval guns. This placed the leaders of the country in his debt and helped Weizmann and his colleagues attain the Balfour Declaration. Lord Balfour was the Foreign Secretary in late 1917; he addressed his historic letter to Lord Rothschild who was the titular head of British Jewry.

Foreign Office
November 2nd, 1917

Dear Lord Rothschild,

I have much pleasure in conveying to you, on behalf of His Majesty's Government, the following declaration of Sympathy with Zionist aspirations which has been submitted to, and approved by, the Cabinet.

His Majesty's Government view with favor the establishment in Palestine of a national home for the Jewish people, and will use their best endeavors to facilitate the achievement of this object, it being clearly understood that nothing shall be done which may prejudice the civil and religious rights of existing non-Jewish communities in Palestine, or the rights and political status enjoyed by Jews in any other country.

I should be grateful if you would bring this declaration to the knowledge of the Zionist Federation.

Yours Sincerely,

Arthur James Balfour

When the Zionists met for their first post-War Congress, there was no question in anyone's mind that Chaim Weizmann should be president. In order to raise the tremendous sums needed for building a homeland, Weizmann created the Keren Hayesod (in the United States it was known first as the United Palestine Appeal and then as the United Jewish Appeal). In the Weizmann Archives in Rehovoth is found this statement:

A State cannot be created by decree but by the forces of a people and in the course of generations. Even if all the governments of the world gave us a country it would only be a gift of words. But if the Jewish people will go and build Palestine, the Jewish State will become a reality — A fact.

Chaim Weizmann
Jerusalem, 30.1.1921

It was over the Keren Hayesod that the followers of Justice Brandeis and the followers of Chaim

Weizmann parted company. Brandeis believed that private capitol would enable the Jews in Palestine to build while Weizmann believed that the entire Jewish people should participate.

In 1921 Weizmann outlined the basic credo on which his complete political and philosophical outlook rested, that only by building facts can the political goals be achieved.

> The Keren Hayesod is the only ammunition we have in our hands. We have no army, no navy and no diplomats. We have to attempt to carry out the two paragraphs of the Mandate. The dead letter must be transformed into living facts. Show your strength and then you will be taken into account. The Arabs will understand us and have to reckon with us. If we do everything possible in order to establish a good and upright Eretz Yisrael, we can remove from our path all obstacles and opponents.
>
> (ibid.)

Throughout the Twenties and the decades following, Weizmann continually had to contend with the British who were not committed to fulfilling the Balfour Declaration or the League of Nations Mandate charging them with helping the creation of the Jewish national home. To many Jews, England bent over backwards to placate the Arabs. And to many Zionists, Weizmann conceded far too much to placate the British. He truly believed in their good intentions and regarded their offenses as temporary lapses. As he wrote in a letter in 1947: "Any other country would have been worse and certainly not better." Still, he came to realize how shameful was British conduct in the post World War II years when they prohibited those who had survived the horrors of Hitler from entering the only country where they were wanted and would feel at home.

In December of 1946 a World Zionist Congress was convoked, the first after the Holocaust and the War. In his address, Chaim Weizmann said:

It was the destiny of our movement to warn Jewry and mankind of the perils to which we were exposed by reason of our dispersion and homelessnes, and our lack of a place, as a nation, among the nations of the world.

He appealed to the British not to violate the covenant with the Jews made by the Society of Nations. Weizmann proclaimed the difficulty in believing that Great Britain would proceed with its anti-Zionist policy, that it would not listen to the Jews' demand for equality among the nations. He went on to show that the Arabs had attained seven independent sovereignties — "they have territory beyond the dreams of avarice, they have great sources of natural wealth. They have emerged unscathed from wars which have devastated us." Nevertheless, Weizmann refused to renounce faith in peaceful solutions and denounced Jews who would resort to terrorist tactics.

Weizmann was not reelected president at this Congress and he felt bitter. But he did not remain divorced from Zionist work. When the United Nations Special Committee on Palestine arrived in Jerusalem, the Jewish Agency asked him to appear. He did and advocated partition.

In October of 1947 Weizmann met with President Truman to urge recognition of the Jewish State without delay. When the United States Ambassador to the United Nations, on the following day, asked the General Assembly to adopt a trusteeship plan to replace partition, Weizmann felt betrayed. Truman was very disturbed and told an aide: "I assured Chaim Weizmann that we are for partition and would stick to it. Find out how this could have happened." When the State was born, Truman recognized it at once and remarked: "The old doctor will believe me now." The State of Israel was proclaimed on May 14, 1948. The next day Weizmann received a message from Ben Gurion and his colleagues:

On the occasion of the establishment of the Jewish State we send our greetings to you, who have done more than any other living man toward its creation. Your stand and help have strengthened all of us. We look forward to the day when we shall see you at the head of the State established in peace. On May 17 news reached Chaim Weizmann that he had been elected President of the new State of Israel.

David Ben Gurion (1886-1973) was the individual who decided to proceed with statehood in May of 1948 even though colleagues and the American Secretary of State strongly urged waiting for a more propitious time. By that time, he already had the political and moral power to act. It had been won by decades of dedication, involvement and leadership. An astute historian of Zionism once observed: "In our generation which had known DeGaulle and Churchill and Roosevelt and Mao and many other immense figures, Ben Gurion certainly rates with all of these and is of that caliber."

Born not far from Warsaw, raised in a *Hovev Zion* home, taught Hebrew as an infant, David Ben Gurion was a Zionist activist as a teenager. Many years later he recalled:

> I can hardly remember a time when the idea of building what we used to call 'Eretz Israel', or the Land of Israel, wasn't the guiding factor of my life. It is no exaggeration to say that at three I had daydreams of coming to Palestine. And certainly from my tenth year on, I never thought of spending life anywhere else.
> *(Memoirs*, Ben Gurion, p.34)

He remembered seeing Herzl when that majestic figure came to his town and thinking that he was the Messiah. In 1906 Ben Gurion arrived in Jaffa determined to be a *halutz* (pioneer). He had great difficulty in finding work, often went hungry, even suffered from malaria. But he would not leave.

The young *halutz* joined a group in the north that undertook to work the land, a swamp or a hill full of boulders, to prepare it for permanent settlers who would follow. They lived cooperatively and organized their own defense.

Ben Gurion left this work in the Galilee to go to Jerusalem to help write and publish the journal of the labor Zionist Movement. He evinced great journalistic talent and all his life thought of himself as essentially a journalist. After several months he and his friend Yitzhak Ben Zvi (second president of the State of Israel) went to Turkey to learn law. They returned home when World War I broke out but, in 1915, they were exiled by the Turks and went to the United States. In a speech given in New York in the Fall of 1915, Ben Gurion told his audience:

> We do not ask for the Land of Israel for the sake of ruling over its Arabs, nor seek a market to sell Jewish goods produced in the Diaspora. It is a Homeland that we seek, where we may cast off the curse of exile, attach ourselves to the soil — that source of quickening, creativeness and health — and renew our native life.
> (*Rebirth and Destiny of Israel*, Ben Gurion,
> p.4)

Ben Gurion remained in America almost three years, then enlisted in the Jewish Legion, and finally returned home.

He tried to persuade all the labor parties to unite. Many of them did, creating a new party called *Ahdut Avodah*. Ben Gurion was elected its head. *Ahdut Avodah* proceeded to cooperate with those pioneers and workers who maintained their independence and to create an over-all Confederation of Labor, the Histadrut. Ben Gurion became its Secretary General.

In the twenties, thirties and forties Ben Gurion not only ran his party and the Histadrut but often traveled to Europe to represent Palestine Labor at Zionist Congresses, in Jewish communities and, with Zionist colleagues, to the British. He was the unofficial head of the *yishuv*. At the 17th Zionist

Congress held in 1931 Ben Gurion was very forthright:

> We do not, as do the Revisionists, give the feckless pledge — 'Elect us and a Jewish majority in Palestine is yours!' No, we warn you, and every Zionist in the world, that so long as we are few and weak, disaster stalks us. There is no easy diplomatic way — but only our own strength, only sacrifice and unceasing effort, only more and surer footholds through Aliyah and work and settlement, everywise and anyhow. That, to us, is the core of Zionist policy, and the essential concomitant is political activity in Britain and Europe and increasingly among Arabs and in the East.
>
> The moral content of Zionism and its necessary practical objects demand a policy of rapprochement and mutual understanding towards the Palestinian Arabs in economics, enlightenment and politics.
>
> (Rebirth and Destiny, p.37)

Because of Arab violence and refusal to work a way-of-living with the Jews, in 1936 the British suggested the partitioning of Palestine. Many Zionists were unalterably opposed. Not Ben Gurion. He believed that a truncated state was better than no state at all. "A Jewish state in Palestine will help in the realization of Zionism more than a British state in the whole of Palestine."

The Partition Plan of 1936 never reached the point of serious negotiations because the Arabs refused to entertain such a solution. Ben Gurion, in the following years, kept urging increased *aliyah*. In

December, 1938, at a meeting of the Jewish Agency Executive in Jerusalem, he proposed:

> We will convene a world Jewish conference in America to declare and implement an *aliyah war*. We will arrange *aliyah* to Palestine on our own responsibility and confront England with the necessity to use force in their fight against aliyah.
>
> (Protocol of Jewish Agency Executive Meeting, December 1, 1938)

On May 27, 1939, Great Britain issued a White Paper which, in essence, abrogated the Balfour Declaration and the obligations assumed under the League of Nations Mandate. Ben Gurion asserted that a Jewish State should now be demanded. When World War II broke out, there was no question that Hitler rather than Britain was the enemy. Ben Gurion formulated the Zionist position: "We will fight with the British against Hitler as if there were no White Paper; we will fight the White Paper as if there were no war."

The British Foreign Secretary, Ernest Bevin, fought the entry of Holocaust survivors into Palestine and was utterly opposed to Zionism and its purposes. In November, 1945, Ben Gurion delivered an address detailing Bevin's errors and he concluded with this:

> The tombs of Jewish millions are still open in Europe, and already Jewish blood is being spilled again on the soil of the Homeland. Jewish farmers and workers in the Plain of Sharon, defending their national cause, have been shot down, and it may be the beginning of a reign of terror. But our

halutzim will not falter, they will face any danger and the mightiest armaments with faith in the justice of their plan and the purity of their ideals. It is not for me to say whether the British citizen and worker empowered Mr. Bevin to treat the Jewish people as he does. But I can give him this reply on its behalf. We have no desire to be killed. We want to live. We believe, despite the teachings of Hitler and his disciples, that Jews too are entitled to live as individuals and as a people, just as much as the British and the rest. But again, like the British, there are things we value above life itself, things for which we are ready to die rather than surrender: freedom to enter Palestine, the prerogative to remake the wastes of our land, and a sovereign Jewish nation in its own Israel.

(Rebirth and Destiny, pp.174-175)

After the UN decision in November of 1947 to create a Jewish state and an Arab state in Palestine, Ben Gurion met with the High Commissioner in Jerusalem. The High Commissioner did not congratulate him, but Ben Gurion expressed the hope that they would part in friendship and asked for his cooperation during the transition period. The representative of His Majesty's Government promised to consider the matter but did nothing until his departure in mid-May.

B. CULTURAL ZIONISTS

Prof. Mordecai Kaplan once began an article on Ahad Haam (1856-1927) with these words: "Asher Ginzberg, whose pen-name was Ahad Haam, is probably the one person in Jewish history who, next to Maimonides, deserves the title of 'Guide for the Perplexed.'" Indeed, this master Hebrew essayist guided many perplexed Jews, taught them and forced them to think about contemporary Jewish problems in new ways. Although his name was Asher Ginzberg, everyone spoke of him only by the modest name he signed to his first essay: Ahad Haam, One of the People.

Until maturity he lived in a pious Hasidic home where he was given an intensive Talmudic education. He acquired his vast knowledge of European thought and languages on his own. When he was thirty, he and his family moved to Odessa for business reasons and here he found an intellectual circle that was congenial. He joined the *Hovevei Zion* and, when asked to write a critique of the movement, he penned his first essay, "*Lo Zeh Haderekh.*" He began by stating the phenomenon that had occurred in Jewish life:

> After many centuries of poverty and degradation on the outside and faith in and hope for the mercies of Heaven within, there has come in our generation a new and promising idea which would bring down from heaven for us the faith and the hope and make them both living, active forces: to establish that hope on earth and that faith on the Jewish people. ...the idea took on the

form of "settling *Eretz Yisrael*" and became a reality.

However, Ahad Haam went on, what was done went awry, that what was needed — before attempts to solve the economic needs of the Jewish people — was a revival of national sentiments and of the Jewish spirit.

The basis of Ahad Haam's thinking was that the Jews were a national group. Personally not religious, he respected religion and observed many religious practices. But he insisted that Judaism was not basically a religion, that religion was but one of the phenomena of Jewish nationalism. This nationalism was not dependent upon either geography or political sovereignty; rather was it based on spiritual and moral foundations. Indeed, every nation possessed a spirit of its own reflected in the national character of the group. In 1910, he wrote to an American rabbi:

"National religion" — by all means. Judaism is fundamentally national, and all the efforts of the "Reformers" to separate the Jewish religion from its national element have had no results except to ruin both the nationalism and the religion. Clearly, then, if you want to build and not destroy, you must teach religion on the basis of nationalism with which it is inseparably intertwined. ...In my view our religion is national — that is to say, it is a product of our national spirit — but the reverse is not true. It is impossible to be a Jew in the religious sense without acknowledging our nationality, it is possible to be a Jew in the national sense without accepting many

things in which religion requires belief.
(Hertzberg, p. 262)

In the 19th century, traditional Judaism began to break down, to be threatened by disintegration and decay. The only way to overcome all the dangers, insisted Ahad Haam, was to establish a *merkaz ruhani*, a spiritual center in *Eretz Yisrael*. That was the only land sacred to all Jews and upon it had been developed the Jewish culture of the past. He did not advocate neglect of the material aspects of life nor a settlement limited to the elite of the Jewish people. But he did assert that the revised Jewish spirit in Palestine would invigorate Jewish life everywhere. The center would exert a spiritual influence on Jews throughout the world, would strengthen Jewish morale, would increase the feeling of unity among Jews and would overcome the negative effects of living in the exile.

In a letter he wrote in 1903, Ahad Haam stated that his idea of a "spiritual center" was not of a small group of Jews spending their days and nights only in study. He understood the realities of life and told his friend:

Palestine will become our spiritual center only when the Jews are a majority of the population and own most of the land. Then they will automatically control the institutions that shape the culture of the country, will impress their own spirit and character on the whole of its life, and will thus create that new pattern of Jewishness which we need so desperately and cannot find in the diaspora.

When Herzl appeared and the World Zionist Organization was established, Ahad Haam did not rejoice. He was always involved in Zionism (he was the mentor of Chaim Weizmann) but as a critic. He did not agree with those who thought that the establishment of a Jewish state would solve all the problems of all the Jews.

Ahad Haam proceeded to analyze the need for Judaism to continue its development after meeting with Western culture but being unable to do so in exile. Judaism

> can no longer tolerate the *Galut* form which it had to take on, in obedience to its will-to-live, when it was exiled from its own country; but, without that form its life is in danger. So it seeks to return to its historic center, where it will be able to live a life developing in a natural way, to bring its powers into play in every department of human culture, to broaden and perfect those national possessions which it has acquired up to now, and thus contribute to the common stock of humanity, in the future as it has in the past, a great national culture, the fruit of the unhampered activity of a people living by the light of its own spirit. For this purpose Judaism can, for the present, content itself with little. It does not need an independent State, but only the creation in its native land of conditions favorable to its development: a good-sized settlement of Jews working without hindrance in every branch of civilization,

from agriculture and handicrafts to science and literature.

(ibid., p. 267)

It is clear from this essay that Ahad Haam never opposed the idea of a state itself. He differed from Herzl in that he saw the Jewish State as the culmination of many years of effort rather than as a beginning. IIis principal concern was saving Judaism; Herzl's was saving Jews. He felt that Herzl was putting the cart before the horse, that his emphasis on saving Jews caused the greater danger to be overlooked: the need to save Judaism.

Ahad Haam was one of the Weizmann's principle advisors in the period of negotiations with Great Britain that culminated with the Balfour Declaration. He warned him against accepting a loosely worded document.

Ahad Haam stressed that it should designate Palestine as a Jewish National Home and not merely state that a Jewish National Home would be established *in* Palestine. He urged that the document prepared for the Paris Peace Conference contain specific authorization of the national-historic rights of the Jewish people. In December, 1918, Ahad Haam wrote Weizman:

> Just a few days ago, you told me that the document for the Peace Conference would contain a specific declaration of the national historic rights of the Jews to *Eretz Yisrael.* However, in place of the word **RIGHTS,** you have carefully stated the word **CLAIMS:** the word **NATIONAL** is left out entirely, and whatever is left is in the form of a clause, as if this authorization, when

considered by itself, is not deserving of a paragraph of itself! However, to me, at any rate, it is clear that this authorization, a clear and specific one, is the thing we most need to achieve at the Peace Conference.

After the Palestine Mandate was granted to Great Britain, there was much discussion over the appointment of a High Commissioner. Many thought that a Jew should be appointed. Ahad Haam keenly saw the lack of wisdom in such a step.

Weizmann later pointed out: "In the Days of the Balfour Declaration he was probably at his best. There the philosopher, the practical man (many forget that Ahad Haam was an eminently able businessman), and the sage were fused into one. His advice, his guidance, his criticism, his caution, were tremendously valuable and tremendously constructive. I did not take a single step without consulting him first. ...His experience was vast. But, above all I treasured his profoundly analytical mind."

In 1922, Ahad Haam moved to Tel Aviv where he was surrounded by old friends and disciples. He was too ill to engage in any serious literary projects. He died on January 2, 1927.

In volume III of Ahad Haam's letters, there is one written to Martin Buber (1878-1965) on January 21, 1902:

I was happy to hear from afar that there has arisen a group of intellectual young people devoted to spiritual nationalist work, and my joy is doubled to see from your letter that you do not just talk but act. May the God of Zion be with you and may you

succeed! I am ever ready to help you in any
way I can...

Buber had written to him to ask permission to
translate his works into German because Buber
regarded him as his teacher. Even though Ahad
Haam's idea of Palestine as a cultural center was not
central to Buber's thinking, Ahad Haam was for him
an authentic Jew who presented a Zionism different
from the purely political doctrine of Herzl. It was his
emphasis on cultural rather than political Zionism that
made Ahad Haam so attractive to the young Buber.

At the same time, Buber was also attracted to
Theodore Herzl, even though he joined Weizmann in
criticizing the founder of Zionism for failing to
include cultural work in the Zionist program. In 1901,
he agreed to serve as editor of the World Zionist
Organization's German newspaper, *Die Welt.* He
continued to believe that the Jewish people should
have their own home in the Land of their Fathers in
order to develop their own spiritual tradition but he
did not want to become further immersed in political
work. He founded numerous Zionist groups and
lectured and wrote on Zionism, always stressing its
spiritual purposes.

Buber was not the secularist that ahad Haam was.
He thought in religious terms becoming later one of
the most eminent religious thinkers of the century. He
argued that it was a mistake to think that

emigration to Palestine alone would
revitalize the Jew. There have been many
indications that a "Galut" could exist in
Palestine as well. Because our liberation
means above all inner clarification, the
meaning of Zionism is that Jews, who are

pure of heart, would be transported to Palestine by their longing for wholesomeness and harmony and by a desire for a radical change in their lives. This is the deepest and truest meaning of Ahad Haam's teachings concerning the preparation of the *Volk* and the restoration of the heart.

(Studies in Zionism, Autumn 1982, p. 179)

Buber had no sympathy with the point of view which urged Jews to be a nation like all other nations. To him Israel is the only nation in the world which, from its earliest beginnings, has been both a nation and a religious community.

One might think that the man who led the struggle for the freedom of India, Mahatma Gandhi, would have certainly appreciated the struggle of the Jewish people to attain freedom for themselves in their own land. The Mahatma, however, did not. In late 1938, he published an article criticizing the Jewish reaction to Hitler and the Zionist attitude towards the Arabs. Gandhi urged the Jews of Germany to launch a campaign of passive resistance to the Nazis rather than flee to Palestine and try to establish a Jewish homeland against the will of the Arabs. This article prompted Buber to reply and his open letter was the definite statement of his position on the Jewish right to Palestine. He began by pointing out that the situation of the Jews under Hitler was in no way comparable to that of the Indians in South Africa. The latter were being deprived of their civil rights but not tortured and murdered. Passive resistance against the Nazis, he pointed out, would be futile.

Buber told Ghandi that the Jewish dispersion without the Land of Israel would not be tolerable, would mean the end of the Jewish people. The Jews could not carry out their Biblical mission without being free in their own soil. Moreover, what did Ghandi mean by asserting that the Arabs owned Palestine?

We considered it a fundamental point that in this case two vital claims are opposed to each other, two claims of a different nature and a different origin which cannot objectively be pitted against one another and between which no objective decision can be made as to which is just, which unjust. We considered and still consider it our duty to understand and to honor the claim which is opposed to ours and to endeavor to reconcile both claims. We could not and cannot renounce the Jewish claim; something even higher than the life of our people is bound with this land, namely its work, its divine mission. But we have been and still are convinced that it must be possible to find some compromise between this claim and the other, for we love this land and we believe in its future; since such love and such faith are surely present on the other side as well, a union in the common service of the land must be within the range of possibility.

Where there is faith and love, a solution may be found even to what appears to be a tragic opposition.

In 1938, Buber left Europe to settle in Jerusalem and to teach at the Hebrew University. He was very concerned about the relations between the Jews and the Arabs, hoping that he could reconcile them. He and his friends and disciples (organized into a group first call "Brit Shalom" and later "Ihud") believed it was possible to create a bi-national state, one in which Jews and Arabs would be equal. But he fully accepted the State of Israel when it was born, saying:

> I have accepted as mine the State of Israel, the form of the new Jewish community that has arisen from the war. I have nothing in common with those Jews who imagine that they may contest the factual shape which his Jewish independence.

C. Labor Zionists

Not all Zionists agreed on the nature of the Jewish state they sought to make a reality. There were those who wanted it to be based on *halacha* and expected all its citizens to follow rabbinic authorities. There were others who expected a Western type state in which a democratic capitalism would prevail. Ahad Haam was concerned with the quality of Jewish life in *Eretz Yisrael* and looked for a rejuvenation of Jewish culture. And then there were those who believed in socialism as well as Zionism and created an ideology that combined both, people who believed that salvation lay in labor.

The latter consisted principally of the *halutzim*, pioneers, who began coming in 1902 to work the soil, to redeem themselves and their people through physical labor. Indeed, they made a religion of labor. The person who affected them most was Aaron David Gordon (1856-1922), a man whose personality and personal example were even more impressive than his writings. Berl Katznelson, one of his younger colleagues, once noted: "Men who lived under the same roof, dug the same furrow and daily saw his ways at home and in the field — regarded him with astonishment and reverence. He seemed to them a human miracle and the paragon of his generations."

Gordon was born into a religious family, studied Bible and Talmud, married and lived a quiet life spending his free time with young people. But, at an age when most people begin to think about retirement, A.D. Gordon embarked on a radically new path. At the age of 48, he decided to go to *Eretz Yisrael* as a *halutz*, a pioneer who would join his younger friends in physical labor. The work was arduous but it uplifted his soul. In a letter to his family back home, he wrote: "I am like a new-born babe; I have been born anew. The work is backbreaking but it gives so much to the soul." In one of his essays, Gordon stated his credo:

> In Palestine we must do with our own hands all the things that make up the sum total of life. We must ourselves do all the work, from the least strenuous, cleanest, and most sophisticated, to the dirtiest and most difficult. In our own way, we must feel what a worker feels and think what a worker thinks — then, and only then, shall we have a culture of our own, for then we shall have a life of our own.

Gordon firmly believed that this was the only way for the Jewish people to regain normalcy and to live a healthy life.

It was the return to Nature that had to be the basis of the return to Zion. Jews were estranged for centuries but could no longer continue being so.

To Gordon, work was not merely a means to get bread or to acquire material things. He saw it as something holy in and of itself, an art, a universal ideal.

One of the terrible indictments, Gordon charged against life in the Galut was its making Jews parasites. The only way to cure that affliction was to return to *Eretz Yisrael* and there engage in labor.

Gordon criticized Ahad Haam's ideas as insufficient. He agreed that it was necessary to infuse Jewish nationalism with Jewish culture but opposed "spiritual renascence" that was limited to the heart and the brain, that was not all-embracing, "giving vitality to the whole body and receiving its vital strength from the whole body."

Gordon was not a Marxist. He did not view society's problem in terms of a class struggle nor the human being as subject to economic processes. He deemed Marxism too mechanical and criticized it for neglecting the individual. Gordon believed that human beings could change conditions by undertaking changes, that they themselves could control society if they wished and were not subject to some force outside themselves. He associated with *Hapoel Hatzair*, the Labor Party that permitted freedom of speech and of conscience, becoming its spiritual father.

Gordon was never anti-Arab but believed that they had forfeited their rights to Palestine because they allowed the land to remain a wilderness; they neither cultivated it nor developed it. He felt that they should have rights if they worked and tended the soil, just as Jews.

Gordon regarded all nations as organs of society, just as individuals are the constituent organs of their nation. Every person is an atom of the body called "nation" and every nation is an atom of society. Therefore, if any nation disappeared all of society suffered. If any nation lived, worked and created all of society benefitted. For this reason, any sick nation needed health and that could be gained only by labor.

The greatest theoretician of the Jewish socialism was Ber Borochov (1881-1917). One of his admirers wrote: "What Karl Marx did for the international labor movement, Borochov did for Jewish labor. He gave it a particular base of operation, an independent role in history, and a definite social goal. And even as Marx, Borochov evolved a methodology..."

Borochov grew up in the Ukraine attending a Russian school rather than a *heder* or *yeshivah* but, despite his brilliance, was denied a gold medal because of anti-Semitism. He was a committed Zionist but he was also attracted to Marxism. He joined the *Poalei Zion* party and, in late 1906, formulated its program which he published under the title "Our Platform." His thinking and even his vocabulary were Marxist but he nevertheless expressed Zionist concepts.

"In Palestine, the Jewish immigrants for the first time not only will aim to satisfy the needs of the native population, but will also produce for the external market of the surrounding countries of the Mediterranean, and in time even for the world market. Until now, Jews have always been dependent upon the native populations in the lands of the galut. The organization of Jewish labor was not self-sufficient but was determined by the nature of the relationships that existed among the native population. The Jewish welfare in the galut was always dependent upon the "usefulness" of the Jews to the ruling nationality. The needs of the natives, their ability to pay, and the rivalry between Jewish merchants and professionals and the corresponding groups of the native population — all of these factors helped bring about a narrowed field for Jewish economy in the galut. Aside from these limitations the Jews, both in their old places of residence and in the new lands of immigration, began to be displaced and become pauperized; they became superfluous. Compulsory isolation became their fate; national oppression and persecutions took place. The chief cause for this one-sided dependence of the Jews on the native population lay in the expatriation of the Jewish people."

Borochov asserted that the Jews could not long remain where they were and had to emigrate. The only place for them to go was Palestine because only there would they be able to take care of their economic needs.

Borochov may have believed in such ideas as the class struggle and inevitable forces of history but not completely. He saw all of these through Jewish eyes and therefore concluded that Zionism was the only way for Jews.

"The landlessness of the Jewish people is the source of its malady and tragedy. We have no territory of our own, hence we are by necessity divorced from nature. Therefore, given the recently developed environment of capitalistic production and competition, this abnormal circumstance quite naturally assumes proportions of an acute and dangerous nature...

For hundreds of years the Jewish masses have blindly searched for a way that will return them to nature, to the soil. At last we have found it. *Zionism is the way.* Zionism is the logical, the natural consequence of the economic revolution that has been going on within Jewish life for the past few hundred years. Even in the Galut, our people have been striving to turn to more "natural" and more productive occupations, but this radical change cannot come to its full fruition in the hostile atmosphere of the Galut. *Zionism is the only movement capable of introducing reason, order and discipline into Jewish life. Zionism is the only answer to the economic and historic need on the Jewish people.*"

(*The Economic Development of the Jewish People*)

In 1906 Borochov was arrested by The Russian government and, when he was let out, he wandered over Europe. In 1907 he helped found the World Confederation of *Poalei Zion* and devoted himself to party activities. He also wrote a great deal, particularly in Yiddish. As time passed, he changed some of his early ideas. He was prepared to rewrite completely his "Our Platform" but death overtook him when he was only 36 years old.

Discussion Questions

1) Zionism, for the purposes of this book, is defined as "an organization aiming to establish a state for Jews in Palestine." (see first paragraph of this chapter) There are many people who call themselves Zionists today. What do you think they mean, or more precisely, what does it mean to be a Zionist today? Compare your definition with the different definitions presented in this chapter.

2) Brandeis explained how being loyal to Israel and America at the same time was not inconsistent. What do you think? Is it hypocritical to have dual loyalties or not?

3) Do you agree with Ahad Haam's statement that "it is impossible to be a Jew in the religious sense

without acknowledging our nationality"? Can one be Jewish and not be a Zionist?

4) Some of the early Zionists, e.g. Ben Gurion, spoke of living with the Arabs peacefully. How do you think they would respond to the situation in Israel today?

Chapter 8

ZIONISM AND THE CONSERVATIVE MOVEMENT

From its earliest days,indeed before it became a distinct movement, Conservative Judaism wholeheartedly embraced the Zionist Idea. Committed to the totality of Judaism, it rejected all attempts to sever the Jewish faith from Jewish peoplehood, insisting that the two were inextricably bound to each other. Prof. Louis Ginzberg clearly enunciated this position:

> Jewish nationalism without religion would be a tree without fruit, Jewish religion without nationalism would be a tree without roots.
> *(United Synagogue Reports* 1913-1919,
> p. 21)

Although there was no Conservative movement as such in the middle of the 19th century, there were spiritual leaders who espoused the concept of tradition and change and are now considered as forerunners of the later movement. Foremost among them was Isaac Leeser (1808-1868), Philadelphia rabbi and educator. For twenty-six years, he edited the journal which he founded, *The Occident*, writing about all Jewish matters and influencing many readers. Leeser believed that God had ordained Palestine for the Jews and therefore the Jews must cultivate its soil. He contributed to all who came to him in behalf of Jews in the Holy Land but repeatedly called on them to become self-supporting rather than reply on charity. Long before the *halutzim* dedicated themselves to the ideal of self-labor, Leeser wrote:

> ... our land is sterile only because the laborers are wanting to cultivate the soil. Encourage the first to work, and let the others feel the furrows of the plough, and the stroke of the spade, and the world will see the valley of Raphaim glowing under a rich harvest, and the plains of Yisre-el covered with the riches increase.
>
> *(The Occident*, March 1853)

Leeser foresaw a renewed Jewry contributing not only to itself but also to the world.

Isaac Leeser's successor as spiritual leader of Philadelphia's Sephardic Mikveh Israel congregation, one of the oldest synagogues in America, was Sabato Morais (1823-1897). It was Morais who founded the Jewish Theological Seminary and served as its first head. As a pious Jew, he believed that *Eretz Yisrael* was the homeland of the Jewish people. In 1890, he said in one of his addresses:

> Palestine will always arouse the deepest respect, not only to the Jew but also to the Christian and Moslem who has studied the history of the Jews. He cannot help but feel respect and appreciation for Palestine the

Land of Beauty. Every grain of its sand carries the stamp of the courage of our people's heroes. There, our prophets declared the words of the Lord. Palestine! Which Moses longed to enter ... there is no doubt that it is the center of the earth in every person's heart. I believe with a perfect heart in the tradition of our fathers and our seers that Israel will dwell securely in Palestine and from there will go forth peace and truth to the entire world. Therefore, it is proper and right for us to do all that we can in behalf of Palestine. ... Raise funds, send healthy people to build new colonies there.

(Hamelitz, March 9, 1890)

When Morais died, the Seminary which he had established was small and feeble. It took on new life and developed into one of the world's foremost academies of learning only with the coming in 1902 of Solomon Schechter (1849-1915) to assume its leadership. Later, Schechter also organized the United Synagogue as the representative body of congregations identified as Conservative.

Schechter's attachment to *Eretz Yisrael* was part of the very air he breathed in his native Rumanian village. In his early years, he often thought of settling there as his twin brother had done. To him, as to all traditional Jews, Zion and Jerusalem were precious.

Still, at first, Schechter did not respond to Theodore Herzl because of the non-religious character of Zionism. He cold not accept a nationalism separated from religion; both were fundamental. In a 1904 letter to Israel Zangwill, Schechter wrote:

I have spent nearly 50 years on the study of
Jewish literature and Jewish history and I
am convinced that you cannot sever Jewish
nationality from Jewish religion.

(Solomon Schechter, Bentwich, p. 312)

Schechter did accept the basic ideas of Ahad
Haam. He corresponded with him and greatly
respected him. At the same time he kept abreast of
Zionist affairs and cared about them. After a while, he
decided that he did want to be part of the Zionist
Organization, that his place was within the Zionist
ranks and he became a member.

In 1905 he wrote a masterful essay, "Zionism: A
Statement," in which he explained his affiliation: "To
me, personally, after long hesitation and careful
watching, Zionism recommended itself to me as the
great bulwark against assimilation." Schechter
perceived that Zionism had saved many Jews who
otherwise would have been lost.

Schechter went on to make clear what his
concept of Zionism was:

I belong to that class of Zionists that lay
more stress on religious-national aspects of
Zionism than on any other feature peculiar
to it. The rebirth of Israel's national
consciousness and the revival of Israel's
religion or, to use a shorter term, the revival
of Judaism, are inseparable.

(ibid, p. 97)

As he neared the conclusion of this seminal
essay, Schechter said that Zionism "is the Declaration
of Jewish Independence from all kinds of slavery

whether material or spiritual." And he voiced his conviction that the future will match the past:

> We know that the Bible which influenced humanity so deeply and proved so largely instrumental in the partial conversion of the world, arose in Palestine or in circles which looked on Palestine as their home. Those who wrote the Bible moved and had their whole being in the religious national idea, and lived under the discipline of the law. History may, and to my belief, will repeat itself and Israel will be the chosen instrument of God for the new and final mission; but then Israel must first effect its own redemption and live again its own life, and be Israel again, to accomplish its universal mission.
>
> (p. 104)

Shortly before he died, Schechter published a collection of his essays, *Seminary Addresses*, and wrote in the preface:

"Zionism was and still is the most cherished dream I was worthy of having. It was beautiful to behold the rise of this mighty bulwark against the incessantly assailing forces of assimilation."

Schechter left an abiding and profound influence upon all of American Jewry and particularly those associated with Conservative Judaism. He and his colleagues were confident that Zionism was an integral part of Jewish life. One of the leaders of American Zionism, Louis Lipsky, wrote many years after Schechter's death:

It was Dr. Schechter...who made the Jewish Theological Seminary an institution for the graduation not only of rabbis, but also of Zionists. Without exception, its rabbis — leaders and workers — have carried the message of Zionism to all parts of America.

(Palestine Yearbook, Vol. 2, p. 451)

The faculty that Schechter assembled shared his views of the Jewish religion and the Jewish people. All were Zionists but most were so occupied with scholarship that they took little part in public affairs. Professor Alexander Marx once testified: "After all, we were all Zionists — but not active." Prof. Louis Ginzberg, in 1919 when he was acting president of the United Synagogue, urged participation in the Zionist enterprise.

I believe that the time has come when the United Synagogue should take an active part in the work for the restoration of Palestine. Most of the members of the United Synagogue, congregations as well as individuals, are enthusiastically engaged in this kind of work, and it is high time that the voice of our organization be heard in a matter so deeply affecting the spiritual life of the Jew.

(United Synagogue Reports 1913-1919 p. 20)

The most active Zionist among those whom Solomon Schechter gathered about him at the Seminary was Israel Friedlander (1876-1920) — eminent Arabist and Bible scholar. Friedlander was not content to live solely in the academic world but took part in communal affairs. He was the first president of Young Judea, one of the founders of Young Israel, a member of the Governing Board of the Intercollegiate Menorah Society. He was a member of the executive of the Federation of American Zionists and chairman of New York Jewry's Bureau of Jewish Education. Friedlander believed that it was possible to create a dynamic American Jewish community while working for a restored Zion, that the two goals were interdependent.

Just as he rejected the extremes of religion or nationalism, insisting instead on religion plus nationalism, so did he reject the proposition of Diaspora or Palestine and insisted on the principle of Diaspora plus Palestine. In suggesting such a synthesis, he wrote that Palestine was:

> indispensable for the continuation of Judaism for it was the only spot where the spirit of Judaism, undisturbed by conflicting influences could develop normally and enfold all.

Friedlander was a devoted disciple of Ahad Haam whose essays he translated into German. He rejected all extremisms. He did not believe that Judaism in the Diaspora could survive if there were no Eretz Yisrael; on the other hand, the establishment of a revived Eretz Yisrael did not mean the end of Diaspora Jewry. In one of his essays (collected in a book entitled Past and Present) he explained that modern Jewry adopted the thesis of Diaspora when it emerged from the ghetto.

> Consumed with the desire for emancipation, for sharing the benefits and attractions of

the new life around them, the Jews discarded the hope for an independent national existence in Palestine, which had been their lode-star throughout the ages. *Diaspora* as opposed to *Palestine*, as exclusive of it, became the slogan of emancipated Jewry. The Jewish religion was refitted to harmonize with this new striving for material and cultural progress. ...

(p. 450)

Having used the technique of thesis, antithesis and synthesis to analyze the Diaspora and Palestine, Friedlander proceeded to analyze the nature of Judaism in the same manner.

From its earliest beginnings down to the time of modern emancipation, Judaism represented an indissoluble combination of nationalism and religion. Though ultimately intended to appeal to the whole of humanity, Judaism was essentially a *national* religion. ...The Jewish people was, first and foremost, a *religious* nation. Its sole reason for existence was, in the belief of its members, "to know the Lord" and to make Him known to others....

("Zionism and World Peace" — a pamphlet)

Friedlander proceeded to show how this development was most noticeable in America where immigrants came from Germany and from Eastern Europe and represented both extreme views. In the freedom of the New World, one might have expected these extremists to have clashed; however, reality has proven the opposite and they have learned to cooperate. Through this cooperation, the different sections came to know one another, to understand one another, and to appreciate the other's views. The German Jews were beginning to appreciate the effects of a Hebraic life in Palestine on the Diaspora and the Russian Jews were helping build a sound Judaism in the New World. Therefore, Zionism should not become identified with any specific sector but should be concerned only with the securing of a Jewish center for the Jewish people as a whole.

Friedlander concluded this keen analysis with a plea for the synthesis which would become the common ground for all.

Representing the common longings of the Jewish people throughout the world, Zionism should serve as a leaven, quickening and stimulating the Jewish activities of this country, and rescue them from the greatest danger of Diaspora Judaism, the danger of provincialism, of falling away from the main body of universal Israel.

Dr. Friedlander coped with the charge of dual loyalties, insisting that there was no conflict between love of country and love of the ancient homeland. Addressing the Eighth Convention of the New York Jewish Community of April 28, 1917, he stated:

The Jewries of the world love their own country, even as a man loves his wife. But *all* the Jewries of the world love, in addition *Eretz Israel*, "the Land of Israel" — even as a man loves his mother. ...A son who is ashamed of his love for his mother makes, indeed, a poor husband."

He continued to assert that the Jew's love for America is purer and deeper because he is also devoted to Palestine. The Jew cannot forget the unusual love for the Promised Land which has persisted despite two thousand years of wandering. As he continued to point out all the achievements of the Return to Zion movement, Friedlander touched upon one of the foundation pillars of Conservative Judaism, the unity of the Jewish people. Indeed, Palestine was all the more precious because it was a symbol of the unity of Israel. It served as such a symbol because it was a center of the Jewish spirit, because

> A portion of our people settled in the Holy Land will prove a focus which will gather the efforts of all the Jewries of the world, and it will prove at the same time a power-house which will send forth its energies to the whole house of Israel.

Thus, Israel Friedlander echoed his mentor, Ahad Haam. Indeed he beautifully captured the essence of Cultural Zionism when he said:

> Rejuvenated Zion, by gathering the scattered energies of Israel, will prove again a great spiritual focus which will send out its vivifying rays to the stiffening limbs of the Jewish national organism throughout the Diaspora and will make Judaism shine forth once more as the luminous bearer of a religious message to humanity.

Being one of the leading exponents of Zionism in the United States Professor Friedlander frequently found himself called upon to engage in polemics with Jewish and non-Jewish antagonists. In these writings, he demonstrated the weakness of his opponents' arguments and clarified the implications of Zionism. Some of his statements, although written nearly half a century ago, sound almost contemporary, such as the one wherein he pointed out that a Jewish state was not an end in itself but a means towards a higher goal:

> It is not an end in itself, an agency for political aggrandizement and the injustice and oppression that goes with it, but it is a means to an end, the physical vessel for a spiritual content, the material agency for the consummation of the great ideals of justice and righteousness. ... Zion is primarily an opportunity for the Jewish people to express itself in accordance with its ancient ideals and aspirations.

Of all the brilliant young scholars whom Solomon Schecter chose to train rabbis who believed in both tradition and change, none had quite the impact that Mordecai M. Kaplan (1881-1983) had. In his long and fruitful life, Professor Kaplan stimulated people to think deeply about the nature of Judaism in both *Eretz Yisrael* and America and about the ways Jews should live their Jewish lives communally and individually. In his later years, some of his disciples, left the Conservative Movement to form the Reconstructionist movement as a separate distinct group. But before and after that break, Professor Kaplan was regarded as *the* great teacher by those who disagreed with his thinking as well as by those who looked upon him as their master.

Long before May 15, 1948, Mordecai Kaplan was already an active Zionist asserting that the Jews were a people who needed a home in Palestine. He was deeply influenced by Ahad Haam, as he once stated:

> For signs of Jewish awakening I had to turn to the Zionist movement, and for evidence that we had begun to adventure beyond the stereotypes of medieval philosophy, I had to turn to Ahad Ha'am with his version of spiritual Zionism.
>
> *(Mordecai M.Kaplan: An Evaluation*, edited by Eisenstein Kohn, p. 298)

Early in his writings Rabbi Kaplan pointed out that the Jews had a special relationship with Zion.

> If we realized to what extent everyone who had anything to do with molding Jewish life centered his efforts upon maintaining the national integrity of the Jewish people, we can understand why we would have to start *de novo* if we were to disassociate Jewish self from Palestine, and form ourselves into a religious organization pure and simple. Whatever regimen of conduct such an organization would adopt, it would not be Judaism.
>
> *(SAJ Review*, May 24, 1929).

Dr. Kaplan attended the Zionist Congress in 1923 and, upon his return, said in an interview:

The Zionist Congress must be regarded as a necessity in Jewish life not only from the point of view of the economic rehabilitation of Palestine, but as a demonstration of the unity and integrity of the Jewish people. We must have a national corporate body which should speak for us. Nothing should be done to undermine the influence of the Congress as an institution in Jewish life. The Congress has come to serve as a school where the Jew is learning his lesson in the art of politics, in the art of getting along with his brother Jew. There he learns to make compromises and to arrive peacefully at an understanding of Jewish problems. Jewish unity is no longer possible without a readiness to compromise.

(*The New Palestine*, September 7, 1923)

The fruit of more than two decades of serious thinking resulted in Kaplan's massive work, *Judaism As A Civilization*, which first appeared in 1934. In this work, he not only analyzed Jews and Judaism but also presented his program for the future. Included in this program was an understanding of the nature of the Jewish group and its relationship to the Land of the Fathers.

He asserted that there was an intimate relationship between a people's country and its social and spiritual life. "What soil is to the life of a tree, a land is to the civilization of a people". However, since there will be a large Jewish community outside the Land of Israel, the status of the Jews will become that of an international nation with a home in Palestine. This will be of great benefit not only to the Jew but to all of society.

Kaplan insisted that Judaism could not continue to function as the civilization of a landless people. To do so would be a severance with its past. The land that is needed could only be the historic land of Palestine. Throughout the ages, it has been the dream and goal of the Jewish people.

This does not mean that all Jews need return to Palestine. It means that Palestine must become the place where the Jewish civilization will be primary. Indeed, Palestine already is a symbol and exerts a cohesive influence on Jewry; it is already creating cultural content.

Judaism As A Civilization was the culmination of years of thinking but it was not the ultimate. Dr. Kaplan did not rest on his laurels, oblivious to all that happened. He continued thinking, teaching and expounding. He formulated his version of the Ahad Haamian concept of the spiritual center, stating that the relationship of *Eretz Yisrael* to world Jewry is that of a hub to the spokes of a wheel. But both are needed if the wheel is to function. The hub alone is insufficient; the spokes without the hub are mere slats of wood. Similarly, Israel and the Diaspora are necessary.

One of the most brilliant disciples of Mordecai Kaplan was Rabbi Milton Steinberg (1903-1950) whose thoughts on Jewish theology and the Jewish people have been highly respected. Steinberg was convinced that Zionism was necessary for meaningful Jewish life. In a pamphlet written in 1945, he stated:

It is not true that I am Zionist because I am not content to be an American. ...In part, I am a Zionist because of the record of Zionist accomplishment. ...And yet I cannot claim it as the ground of my conviction. For, truth to tell, I was of my present persuasion before that record was achieved. ...I am a Zionist in the first place because I am a religious Jew. From my Judaism I have derived a God Faith, an ethical code, personal and social, a pattern of observances, but, also, interwoven with these, a love for Palestine and the yearning that at least a part of the House of Israel be restored to its soil. ...My religious heritage, then makes me a Zionist.

(The Creed of An American Zionist)

Steinberg went on to show that whenever the Jewish people struck roots in Palestinian soil, it produced great things. The first time, the Bible was the result; the second time, Rabbinic Judaism, Christianity and the beginning of Islam resulted. Now, with the third encounter, we can expect something new and equally as great. And, he continued:

The brilliant renaissance in Palestine, the revival there of Jewish music, art, letters, folkways, the theater, and the Hebrew tongue have invigorated, stimulated and enriched every Jewry in the world. That too is why I am a Zionist; because, while I would remain a Jew without Jewish Palestine, my Judaism, by virtue of it, is more meaningful to me and my Jewish fellows.

In an even earlier essay, Rabbi Steinberg pointed out that Palestine is a matter of personal concern to American Jews if their cultural sources are not to become obsolete.

For Palestine is the one place in the world where a Jew is a Jew without the necessity of being something else first. Only there is Judaism the primary culture of the Jews. It is to Palestine then that we must look with greatest hopefulness for novel creation. ...The Jewish life of every Jew in America is the richer and the fuller because of Palestine.

(The Place of Palestine in Jewish Life)

He continued with the warning that the growth of a new Jewish life in *Eretz Yisrael* did not exempt American Jews from building an adequate Jewish life on the American scene. It simply meant the possibilities of a fuller and richer life. Moreover, it had great psychological value. A member of a minority inevitably feels at times that he is an outsider. A Jew feels himself penalized economically and socially and may regard his Judaism as frustrating. The result may be a resentment against his Judaism which he cannot escape but which can be regarded as crippling. Palestine, however, bestows a sense of normalcy and meaning to the individual's Jewish life. It provides a positive program, actions which make life significant, inspiration that results in a sense of inner worth.

In his *The Making of the Modern Jew*, which appeared in 1943, Steinberg pointed out that the appearance of Zionism on the modern scene was indeed a miracle. He considered it the greatest single factor making for Jewish survival and opening up new vistas of hope and rebirth. Feeling that *Eretz Yisrael* had already begun to serve as a spiritual center, he commented:

...out of the vitality of Palestine Jewry revivifying influences have passed to the Diaspora. Judaism in all lands have been stimulated by a transfusion of energy.

In a later work, *A Partisan Guide to the Jewish Problem*, published in 1945, Milton Steinberg again asserted that the record of Jewish accomplishments in Palestine has already justified Zionist efforts. Moreover, the hope for future accomplishments was even greater.

Living in the forties, when European Jewry had been destroyed and the miserable survivors needed rescue and rehabilitation, Steinberg repeatedly urged that Jews be rescued from the torment of Europe and be given the opportunity to participate in the rebuilding of the homeland. When asked to speak for the Women's Division of the United Jewish Appeal, he agreed and delivered one of his most moving addresses: "When I think of Seraye." He dealt there with the survivors of the catastrophe and spoke of the role of the Jewish National Home, stating that it was

an enterprise which has revived, enriched, cleansed and modernized, for the benefit of *all* its inhabitants, a land long poverty-stricken, sterile, retarded and disease-ridden; which has established an outpost of political and economic democracy in the feudal medievalism of the Near East; which has blazed trails towards more equitable and cooperative forms of group life; which has evoked an infinitely rich and colorful revival of Hebraic culture; which has converted Jews like the survivors of Seraye from pauperism to stalwart self-reliance, from a burden to themselves and a problem to the world into a social asset for all mankind.

(A Believing Jew)

It was not only the individual leaders of Conservative Judaism who wrote and taught about *Eretz Yisrael's* centrality in Jewish thinking and living. The group collectively took a stand. In 1938 the Rabbinical Assembly of America adopted this "Pronouncement of Zionism":

I The Zionist ideal to establish in Palestine a legally assured and publicly recognized home for the Jewish people, has been and integral part of the religious outlook as well as of the program of practical activities sponsored by the Rabbinical Assembly of America from its very inception. ...

II We conceived of a Jewish National Home in Palestine as the place where the following conditions could obtain:

A) The maximum possible freedom of entry and residence for Jews from all countries of the world and who for any reason may want to make their home there.

B) The emancipation of Jewish life from the many difficulties inherent in living everywhere as a minority group. This would make possible the free application of all aspects of Jewish religious tradition to all phases of human activity, and the untrammeled natural development of the whole of the Jewish cultural heritage with its distinct language, literature, and manner of life. Such a freely developing Jewish community would then serve as a mighty centripetal force giving sorely needed strength and reality to the spiritual bonds which unite the widely dispersed Jewish communities. It would be for them an inexhaustible reservoir of inspiration, whence would flow those streams of living waters which would prevent the possible petrification or ultimate decay of the Jewish spiritual heritage in their midst.

C) A political government based upon the ethical teachings of our religion...

IV We desire to re-affirm our faith in our religious tradition which has always associated with Palestine the fulfillment of the Scriptural promise; "In thee shall all the nations of the earth be blessed." This promise succinctly but adequately expresses our conception of Zionist aspiration and the national destiny of our people.

V We re-affirm our historic claim to Palestine, as the land where for more than a thousand years our fathers lived a national life and built a religious civilization which has profoundly and beneficently influenced the course of history. ...

The Pronouncement continued to cite the events which gave encouragement that justice would be done, such as the Balfour Declaration and United States Congress resolutions. It affirmed the justice of the Zionist ideal and proceeded to show why the Jewish settlement of Palestine was a necessity. It furthermore urged that the Zionist program be carried out in keeping with the ideals and practices of the Jewish tradition. The Pronouncement concluded with this final paragraph:

> It was an act of brute violence which drove the Jews out of Zion. Only through an act of justice will they be restored. Firm in their faith that justice will ultimately and inevitably triumph in the world, the members of the Rabbinical Assembly reassert their faith in the ultimate triumph of Zionism.
>
> *(Proceedings of the Rabbinical Assembly*
> *1933-1938,*
> pp. 388-400)

The birth of the State of Israel led the leaders of the Conservative movement to probe even more deeply its meaning for Conservative Judaism. When the State was little more than a year old, the president of the Rabbinical Assembly, Rabbi David Aronson, urged that the synagogue should reflect the effect of Israel on the Jewish religion by abolishing the second day of *yomtov* to "serve as a popular symbol of de-jure recognition of the blessed fact of Zion reborn."

Furthermore, he went on:

> I see many reasons for the reorganization and mobilization of our Zionist activities into a special department of the United Synagogue, as an integral part of our

Conservative movement and our religious experience.

(1949 *Proceedings of the Rabbinical Assembly*, p. 130)

Rabbi Aronson indicated that Conservative Jews could not make their contribution as religious Jews through the Orthodox parties, that they have something unique to offer. Therefore, he recommended that

the convention authorize the appointment of a joint commission of the Rabbinical Assembly and the United Synagogue to study ways and means of organizing a religious [Conservative], Zionist wing, with our synagogues as local chapters, and affiliated with whatever federation of American Zionist organizations there will be established as well as with the World Zionist Organization.

(ibid., p. 132)

Rabbi Aronson's suggestion was not acted upon immediately, but he sowed the seeds for future decisions and actions. In 1958, at the convention of the Rabbinical Assembly, a symposium was presented on the theme: "Ideological Evaluation of Israel and the Diaspora". The two participants were Prof. Abraham Joshua Heschel and Prof. Mordecai Kaplan. The former began by setting forth the very wonder of the State of Israel:

Dark and dreadful would be our life today without the comfort and the joy that radiate out of the land of Israel. Crippled is our people, many of its limbs chopped off, some of its vital organs torn out — how strange to be alive, how great is our power to forget. Like a flash-light in the darkness of history came the State of Israel. It is a haven of refuge for those in despair who cried for a sign that God is not forever estranged from the world of history.

We stand at a climax of Jewish history, and what we witness surpasses our power of comprehension and appreciation. We are a generation which has the evidence of the mystery of Israel, but we do not know how to testify.

The question is not how to make the State meaningful to the Jews of America but how to make the State worthy of 2,000 years of waiting. A mysterious relationship obtains between the Jewish people and the Jewish land which remained throughout the ages a challenge to the Jews. It is an essential part of our destiny, and of God's vision of the Messianic kingdom — one cannot detach himself from the land without upsetting one's position within the Covenant. The political and economic realities of the State must not be allowed to obscure that mysterious relationship.

(Proceedings, p. 118)

He proceeded to make clear that aid for the state of Israel was not only a necessity but a privilege and that the religious, spiritual dimensions of Judaism dare not be neglected.

Speaking from the same dais Prof. Kaplan stated:

Zionism occupies an important place in the agenda of our conventions. That means that Zionism is with us not merely a peripheral but a central interest. The fact is that the Zionist movement and the Conservative movement are organically related to each other. That is not the case with either Orthodoxy or Reform. When, therefore, I had occasion recently to address the National Executive Committee of the ZOA, I did so from the standpoint of the Conservative movement.

(ibid., p. 138)

He went on to point out that Zionism was not simply philanthropy. The survival and security of the State of Israel depended not only on relief but, even more, on world opinion and "world opinion will ultimately depend upon what the State of Israel will mean to the Jews." Thus, the most urgent task for Jews was their reeducation. Dr. Kaplan proceeded to present the case for mutual responsibility between Jews in *Eretz Yisrael* and those without. He added that the best instrument for achieving this was the Zionist movement and that religious bodies should join the World Zionist Organization to help create one Jewish people.

It would serve both as a challenge and as an opportunity to our religious denominations to find in the immediate purpose of the Zionist movement a common bond of unity. That purpose is the establishment of an internationally recognized and secure home for the Jewish people in *Eretz Yisrael*. The importance of building bridges between

Eretz Yisrael and the Diaspora is generally recognized. It is no less important, however, to build bridges between the different denominations into which Jewry is divided. At present the only occasion for their coming together is created by the force of anti-Semitism. In Zionism, if it accepts responsibility for reconstituting the Jewish people, the different denominations would be united by a common religious or spiritual bond.

(ibid.)

In 1959 there was a strong debate on the issue of the United Synagogue actually joining the World Zionist Organization. There was a strong position, not because of objections to Zionism but fear that such a step would impinge upon the primacy of the synagogue in Judaism. An exciting symposium was held with Prof. Kaplan and Dr. Nahum Goldman arguing for such an affiliation and Professors Simon Greenberg and Abraham Heschel opposing it.

Dr. Kaplan had already come out with a call for a "New Zionism" and, before the assembled convention, repeated in vigorous terms his conviction that the unity of the Jewish people, essential to its survival and its purpose, needed strengthening. That was the chief reason for the United Synagogue to become officially identified with Zionism — to prove that what united it with the rest of world Jewry overshadowed what divided it. Indeed, he held, the very existence of the Jewish people required the identification of all the Jewish religious forces with Zionism.

Only thus can the common concern of all Jews for the State of Israel as the homeland of Judaism demonstrate the spiritual unity of the Jewish people. Only thus can that concern help world Jewry retain its spiritual solidarity.

(*United Synagogue Proceedings*, 1959, p. 56)

Prof. Kaplan pointed out that the Orthodox were, so far, the only religious force identified with Zionism while the Conservative and Reform remained aloof from the political movement. However, Zionism was and continued to be more than a political movement; it was one which called for the resumption of national life in *Eretz Yisrael* in order to foster to the fullest the Jewish spiritual culture. It made it possible for the Jews to be a history-making people.

A common territory is to the life of a people what a catalyst is to a chemical compound. It brings about an interactivity among all the elements in a people's life and fuses them into an organic unity.

(ibid., p. 60)

Not satisfied with theoretical exposition alone, Dr. Kaplan proceeded to offer a specific platform that would clearly state the Conservative viewpoint regarding the relationship of Judaism to Zionism.

The Conservative movement in Judaism from its very inception has regarded the fulfillment of the goals of the Basel Platform as indispensable to the creative survival of the Jewish people and the future of Judaism.

Coordinate with the establishment of the State of Israel has been its recognition of the need for world Jewish unity.

The World Zionist Organization which has been dedicated to the fulfillment of the Basle program has been the main symbol of world Jewish unity since the beginning of the Jewish emancipation [legal equality, first granted in France in 1791]. If the WZO is to continue as such a symbol, the Conservative Movement advocates the addition of the following principles in its platform.

1. The existence of a democratically organized, spiritually sensitive and politically and economically secure State of Israel is indispensable to the creative survival of the Jewish people and the future of Judaism.

2. The creative survival of the Jewish people is predicated on the assumption that its unity is not of a political character but of an ethnic, cultural and spiritual character.

3. Therefore coordinate with the concern of the World Zionist Organization for the State of Israel should be its concern for the fostering of that spiritual unity.

(ibid., p.61)

On the basis of that platform, Prof. Kaplan urged the Conservative movement to affiliate with WZO.

Rabbi Simon Greenberg, after agreeing to the need for an organization which would mobilize support for Israel and strengthen Jewish unity, disagreed that the WZO was the proper instrument for those goals. Since being a Jew depended upon eligibility for membership in a synagogue, the unity of the Jewish people was a religious rather than a political or ethnic matter. The United Synagogue recognized and fostered all the various aspects of Judaism but it could not be part of an organization that did not give primacy to the Jewish religion.

We see in the establishment of the State of Israel not only the response to the cry of the *Jewish heart* for a life of human dignity, creativity and security, but also a response to the longing of the *Jewish soul* for *kirvat elohim*, for the nearness of God, and the Kingdom of God upon this earth.

(ibid., p. 74)

While calling for spiritual bridges between Israel and American Jewry, Dr. Greenberg stressed that the synagogue was in no way subordinate to the state. Therefore, the United Synagogue could not join any organization which relegated the synagogue to a secondary role or even to that of one among equals. "At no time should the synagogue, as such, become but *another member* of a group whose chief concern is *not* the synagogue."

The debate did not lead to action. The written records only present the arguments and those privy to the behind-the-scenes discussions have not written about them. Thus, we only know that the United Synagogue did not pursue the matter at that time and consequently did not attempt to enter the World Zionist Organization. Individual membership in one of the existing Zionist organizations continued to be encouraged; official Conservative representation in the WZO was not discussed further for some time. Five years later, at the 1964 convention of the

Rabbinical Assembly, Rabbi Greenberg gave a major address on the theme of Israel and the Jewish religion.

> Our religious commitment recognizes *yishuv Eretz Yisrael* [settlement of the land of Israel] to be among the greatest of the *mitzvot*, even as is the practice of *tzedakah* or the study of Torah. The Conservative movement always has identified itself with all efforts that encourage and help Jews to settle in or at least to visit *Eretz Yisrael*. We must recognize the fact that, as a movement, we have not done nearly enough in this area, and there is little comfort in the fact that nobody else in the United States has done very much either. At no time, however, did the Conservative movement directly or indirectly identify itself with any formulation of Zionist philosophy or Jewish theology which looked to or hoped for the complete liquidation of the Jewish communities of the Diaspora regardless of the conditions prevailing in any given community. The problem of the relationship of the Jewish community in the United States to the Jewish community in *medinat Yisrael* [the State of Israel] is one which takes on increasing importance with the passing of every year.
>
> *(Proceedings of the Rabbinical Assembly,*
> 1964, p. 61)

Dr. Greenberg then went on to assert that Conservative Jews could no longer remain neutral in matters affecting the character of the Jewish community in Israel. He called for a recognition of the need to alter the movement's recognition of Orthodoxy aloud, and Israel allowing it to be the government supported religious establishment. The leaders of the Conservative movement had not thus far spoken out against that situation but the time had come to deal with it. Therefore, the Conservative movement must have strong personal and spiritual ties with *Eretz Yisrael* and the Jewish community in the State of Israel. Because of our faith that the message, scope and vitality of the Jewish religion will be immeasurably enhanced by facing up to the problems resulting from its being the religion of a Jewish community enjoying the advantages and carrying the responsibilities of being the majority population of a self-governing state, we must be there as a movement to experience directly the day to day religious problems presented by the new situations and to make our contribution towards their creative solution.

(ibid., p.63)

Thus, the question of the formal relationship of the Conservative movement and the World Zionist Organization became a more urgent question than before. There were those who advocated that the United Synagogue become a constituent of the WZO while others argued that it should be only a consultant organization. The former eventually won. In the Fall of 1976, the World Council of Synagogues (the international organization of Conservative congregations) voted unanimously to join the WZO. Its resolution, adopted on September 15, declared:

At this juncture in the affairs of the State of Israel and of the position of the Jewish people in the world, we want to reaffirm our identification with the goals of Zionism by accepting the invitation of the World Zionist Organization to join its ranks officially as a movement through our international organization, the World Council of Synagogues.

We shall continue to be guided in our Zionist activities by laying 'stress on the religious-national aspects of Zionism', as did Dr. [Solomon] Schechter.

We applaud the increasing emphasis being placed by the World Zionist Organization upon the need to strengthen Jewish learning and Jewish commitment throughout the world.

We reaffirm our commitment to the principle of the legitimacy of religious pluralism for all people, within the Jewish community in Israel and elsewhere, and recognize that the World Zionist Organization has historically provided a platform for all who share the Zionist ideal, although they may differ in their religious and political views....

The time had come to create a Conservative Zionist party. In telling how it came about, Rabbi Gordis wrote:

We are not asking the Orthodox religious establishment to recognize the legitimacy of Conservative Judaism. Not being afflicted with an inferiority complex we neither need nor want it. What we call for is that the State of Israel recognize the equal rights of all interpretations of the Jewish religion and accord freedom to all Jews to share equally in the rights and privileges of Israeli citizenship. In the religious field it means freedom from harassment and insult for the religious institutions. It means support for the professional leadership of Conservative congregations, their schools and adult education programs. We want to cease being spiritually homeless in Zion and demand that the process relegating us to second-class citizenship in the Jewish people be halted and revised.

(Conservative Judaism, Spring 1977, pp. 12-13)

On November 2, 1978 Mercaz was born. A convocation was held at the Jewish Theological Seminary, a rabbi spoke of the integrality of Zionism in the Conservative understanding of Judaism, the Chancellor of the Seminary delivered a supporting statement, and a past president of the United Synagogue spoke. Mercaz became an affiliate of the American Zionist Federation and thus an equal partner of all the other Zionist bodies. It became a separate movement for those wishing to become members. It was not an existing body representing the Conservative congregations but an organization which embodied the Conservative view of Zionism.

As Franklin D. Kreutzer, International President of United Synagogue of America has said, "The Conservative Movement was always in the forefront when it came to Zionist ideals and goals. Now the legacy of Solomon Schechter, first President of the United Synagogue of America, is being implemented in new and exciting ways. Our recent historic emergence on the Zionist scene in a reinvigorated fashion is already being felt. Our participation in the last Zionist Congress in 1987, our commitment to Israel programs and our dedication to pluralism in a democratic society are examples of the role we have and are planning in the future."

In the by-laws which were adopted Article Three states the objectives of Mercaz:

The objects of Mercaz are:
(a) to strengthen Israel and Zionism and to provide and organization through which Conservative Jews may implement and fulfill their Zionist ideals and commitments.
(b) to encourage, as an integral part of K'lal Yisrael, the solidarity of Jewish people in all lands.
(c) to foster the development of Conservative Judaism in Israel, to reaffirm commitment to pluralism in Jewish religious life and to promote the acceptance of such pluralism by the State of Israel so that Conservative Jews may practice Judaism equally with other religious factions.
(d) to promote individual and group aliyah from within the ranks of Conservative Judaism in the United States.
(e) to adopt, from time to time, a platform of Zionist principles which shall include statements on the unity of the Jewish people, the centrality of the State of Israel, the encouragement of aliyah and other Zionist issues.

(f) to maintain affiliation with the American Zionist Federation, Inc., the World Zionist Organization and such other organization as may be appropriate to effectuate these objects.

(g) to cooperate with the United Synagogue of America, its affiliated organizations and constituent arms and other agencies of Conscrvative Judaism in fulfillment of these objects.

The thirty first World Congress took place in 1987. As Evelyn Auerbach, President of Women's League described it:

The year is 1987...90 years [after the first Zionist Congress] ...I enter the **Binyanay Ha'umah** (the national convention-center auditorium) in Jerusalem. I am in the present but also in the past. History haunts me, but my thoughts must project into the future. We need an infusion of new ideas, new interests, new people, new methods of operation, in a word — CHANGE. However, tradition dies hard, habits are difficult to break.

The name of the game is politics, not unknown to us, with its usual jockeying for position (this time, perhaps, played out more intensely). MERCAZ...is privileged to have 20 US and two Canadian delegates. In addition, the World Council of Synagogues...has 15 North American representatives and an Argentine rabbinical student; with alternates and observers we number 85....

Throughout the intense days and nights of the Congress we forego sleep, food and bodily comfort in order to caucus and attend sessions. We are leaving an imprint on Zionism. Conservative...Judaism is changing the course of Zionist history. Tov Me'od.

(Women's League Outlook, Winter 1987, p. 4)

Mercaz emerged as a strong force in persuading the Congress to adopt a resolution calling on Israel to give equal status to all religious movements in Israel.

The World Zionist Congress, representing the Jewish people as a total, shall call for granting complete equality of rights to all streams of Jewish religion, and giving their rabbis the legal right to perform all life cycle events and other rabbinic functions, so that they may work together with all who combat that spiritual malaise that threatens world Jewry as a whole and Israeli society in particular.

When Mr. Simon Schwartz, president of Mercaz (and former president of United Synagogue) was asked in an interview to comment on the full support given the delegation of every arm of the Conservative movement, he replied:

Even during my four years as president of United Synagogue, where a primary goal was unity and cooperation within the movement, there was no occasion when we were more unified than were the joint delegates of Mercaz and World Council of Synagogues at the 31st World Zionist Congress. Maintaining that unity must be one of our Movement's primary concerns we were able to go to the Congress in the strength we did because of our successful membership efforts and success in the election. This was made possible because of meaningful support by the Chancellor of the Jewish Theological Seminary; the resources, structure and leadership efforts of the United Synagogue of America; the efforts of the leadership of the Rabbinical Assembly and many of its congregational rabbis; the support of the women of the Sisterhoods, actively elicited by the leadership of the Women's League for Conservative Judaism; the efforts of the leadership and membership of the Federation of Jewish Men's Clubs; and the superb support of USY.

It is in regard to that support that Hindy Kisch, the administrator of Mercaz, wrote to USYers:

Let me give you an example of how MERCAZ can have an effect on USY. Most of you have had some contact with one of the 3 USY Shalichim who are in the States. The Shalichim provide an important component to USY-Israel programming. They travel within their own regions as well as neighboring regions to assist in all matters relating to Israel and youth. They care. They are involved. They are here to make the bridge between Conservative youth in America and Israel a stronger and more intimate one.

Yet, the USY movement, with a membership of over 17,000, has only 3 Shalichim in America. Other Jewish youth organizations, with far smaller memberships, get 10 or 12 shalichim. Why? Because MERCAZ isn't strong enough....

Here is where you come in, and where YOU can help turn things around and play a part in MERCAZ' present and future. How? simply by becoming a member in MERCAZ. All USY seniors, once they become 18, are eligible for membership. A number of MERCAZ members have set aside money for a scholarship fund to enroll USYers as they become 18. By becoming MERCAZ members you will become knowledgeable about the issues..., and can begin to take a leadership role in bringing about hoped for changes.

(Achshav, Fall 1986, p. 14)

There is still another body which was created in 1982 to raise funds for the movement in Israel: the Foundation for Conservative (Masorti) Judaism in Israel. The Foundation was formed to work closely with all constituents of the Masorti movement and to help both existing and future programs. The Masorti movement (as opposed to the Foundation) was incorporated February 12, 1979. To make its purpose known seven objectives were adopted.

1. To advance Jewish values in Israel and to safeguard and develop Jewish tradition in its historical continuity.

2. To encourage devotion to the Torah in accordance with its developing historical interpretation.
3. To deepen the sense of identity with *Eretz Yisrael* as the homeland of the Jewish people and in the Jewish people's efforts to build and strengthen the State of Israel; and to work for Israel's well being and for the encouragement of aliyah.
4. To integrate Jewish values and ways of life with those of our times; to nurture Jewish values as they are expressed in tradition and in accordance with the needs of the State.
5. To encourage and nurture scientific research into our spiritual and cultural heritage.
6. To strengthen our ties with all the people of Israel by encouraging Jewish brotherhood in Israel and by the maintaining of close ties with Jewish communities throughout the world.
7. To aid our brothers in distress, wherever they may be as an expression of the unity of the Jewish people.

The need to formulate the philosophy of Conservative Judaism became more intense as the years passed. Finally, the distinguished teacher of not only hundreds of congregants but also of rabbis for many decades, Professor Robert Gordis, was asked to head a Commission that would formulate a Statement of Conservative Ideology. That Commission would include rabbis, laymen (including Franklin Kreutzer, current president of United Synagogue) and representatives of the Seminary faculty.

In 1988 the commission presented its conclusions in a small book called *Emet Ve-Emunah*. In the section entitled "The State of Israel and the Role of Religion", *Emet Ve-Emunah* declares:

> The State of Israel, founded for the entire Jewish people, must in its actions and laws provide for the pluralism of Jewish life. The State should permit all rabbis, regardless of affiliation, to perform religious functions, including officiating at marriages, divorces, and conversions....
> Without being a theocracy, Israel should reflect the highest religious and moral values of Judaism and be saturated with Jewish living to the fullest extent possible in a free society.
>
> (p.35)

After affirming the Conservatives' faith that the State of Israel would be a strong, secure, democratic nation that would serve as a haven of refuge for Jews fleeing oppression and a home for all choosing to go on *aliyah*, the statement avers:

> We do not view Israel as just another state or political entity; rather we envision it as an exemplar of religious and moral principles, of civil, political and religious rights for all citizens regardless of race, religion, ethnic origin or sex. We believe that the litmus test of the character of a democratic Jewish state is its treatment of or an attitude towards its religious and ethnic minorities....Israel reborn provides a unique

opportunity for the Jewish people to be a holy people and a blessing to the nations. Consequently it behooves Israel to set an example for other nations to build their societies on the principles of social justice, righteousness, compassion, and love for all citizens of all faiths and ethnic groups.

(pp. 36-37)

The recognition of the State of Israel is associated with equal commitment to Zionism.

We staunchly support the Zionist ideal and take pride in the achievement of the State of Israel in the gathering of our people from the lands of our dispersion and in rebuilding a nation. The State of Israel and its well-being remain a major concern of the Conservative movement as well as all loyal Jews.

(p.38)

It is due to this position that USY sponsors a six-week Israel Pilgrimage every summer. The following are some responses by USYers to the program.

15 REASONS TO GO TO ISRAEL THIS SUMMER
by Reuven M. Lerner

You might be thinking of going to Israel this summer. If so, terrific! You've made a decision which you will never regret. If not, take a look at this list. Maybe one (or more) reasons below will convince you that this summer is the time to be in Israel — not next summer, or next year, even. **This** summer is for Israel.

Why should you go to Israel this summer?

- *To celebrate the 40th anniversary of the founding of the State of Israel along with millions of other Jews.*
- *To learn our history in person, rather than from books.*
- *To show that Jews are willing to support Israel, even when the rest of the world is not.*
- *To experience the thrill of looking out from Massada and seeing the beauty of the morning sun.*
- *To see the sheep at Kibbutz Hanaton.*
- *To improve your Hebrew by speaking with Israelis, instead of your Hebrew teacher.*
- *To see Yad LaKashish and Ma'on Latinok, two tzedakot which you will never forget.*
- *To walk along the same roads as Jews did 2,000 years ago, knowing that not one of our enemies has ever wiped us out.*
- *To eat felafel until you can eat no more.*
- *To see that Israel is not just a land of the past, but a land of the future...with scientific and medical advances equal to or better than any other country.*
- *To help Israel not only with your money, but with your body and soul, as well.*
- *To find out that archaeology is fun and exciting, and lots of hard work.*
- *To lay out on the beaches of Eilat, and learn what a sunburn* **really** *is.*

- *To fulfill the dream that Jews have always had — of returning to the Jewish State, Israel.*
- *Because it's there.*

(Achshav, Spring 1988, p. 7)

COME SEE FOR YOURSELF
by Jay Michaelson

Last year, I went on USY Israel Pilgrimage, and experienced Israel for myself.... Israel does indeed have its good points and its bad points. However, in enumerating what I didn't like about Israel, a feeling of 'danger' wouldn't make the list. Danger from the FOOD, maybe (Israel is renowned for causing rather persistent problems...) but certainly not from any sinister guerilla force. To me, the most dangerous person I dealt with during my six weeks in Israel was a non-English speaking taxi driver. Now THAT'S dangerous. Seriously, USY, like most tours, is so deliberately over-protective, that we had nothing to worry about. Israel must be experienced — and ultimately, judged, — on an individual basis.

(Achshav, Spring 1988, p.9)

With full support for Zionism and the State, *Emet Ve-Emunah* recognizes that there will always be Jews living outside of Zion. There are Diaspora Jews who furnish vital economic, political and moral support to Israel while Israel imbues them with pride and self-esteem.

Some see the role of *Medinat Yisrael* as the cultural and religious center of world Jewry. Others insist that since the days of the Prophets, various foci or centers of Jewish life and civilization in both Israel and the Diaspora, have sustained the creative survival of *Am Yisrael* and *Torat Yisrael.*

The notion that a Hebrew-speaking Jew who lives in Israel can dispense with religion is false. We are convinced that Jewish religion is essential as a source of ethical and moral values....Israel is challenged to maintain, preserve and enhance Jewish moral values and ethical standards, as well as its uniquely Jewish character....

Both the State of Israel and Diaspora Jewry have roles to fill; each can and must aid and enrich each other in every possible way; each needs the other. It is our fervent hope that Zion will indeed be the center of Torah and Jerusalem a beacon lighting the way for the Jewish people and for humanity.

(pp. 39-41)

Thus, *Emet Ve-Emunah* is the latest and most comprehensive statement of the Conservative Movement's philosophy of both God, the Jewish people and Torah.

Discussion Questions

1) If you were to summarize the position of the Conservative movement regarding Zionism and Israel, how would you do it? Do you agree with your

summary? Compare this with *Emet ve Emunah*.

2) What do you think *the* Conservative approach should be to respond to the Arab-Israeli conflict? Is it proper to ask for *the* approach or can there be a variety of approaches?

3) How does the Conservative position on Israel reflect the rabbinic sources quoted in chapter II? Does the movement agree or disagree with the rabbis?

CLOSING REMARKS

The sources here have been culled from Jewish literature written over a span of millennia. They represent different schools of thought, different approaches to Jewish life, to God, to the Jewish people. Regardless of the historical period or philosophical orientation, leaders and ordinary people all looked upon *Eretz Yisrael* as *moledet*, homeland. This was in both a physical and spiritual sense. Each spoke of that homeland with tremendous affection and overwhelming love. Each reflected the conviction that the People of Israel and the Land of Israel were bonded together for all time.

This is the reason that the State of Israel plays the role it does in the life of Jews, even of those who may not even visit there. Israel represents a kind of fulfillment together with a buoying up of hope. It is not simply by chance that there is great interest in archaeology in Israel. Whatever is learned about the past is not merely of academic interest, more facts to be taught in a specialized university classroom. Rather are the findings on unveiling of a part of one's identity, a better understanding of one's past. Berl Katznelson once said: *Im yesh avar, atid gam yesh,* "If there is a past, then there will also be a future."

So, Israel's birth was not only the result of the Holocaust of the 20th century but the fruit of all of Jewish history. Moreover, its birth and continued existence has been a promise. It is an opportunity to build a future in which Jews will not be subject to the whims of others but will be able to rejuvenate the Jewish civilization.

Therefore, each birthday is an occasion to express gratitude and the 40th is a very special one. Our sages said that the age of 40 is one of understanding. The 40th birthday of Israel should be an occasion not only to pray that its leadership be blessed with the understanding necessary to enable the citizens to live in peace and goodness but also one for all of us to understand the importance of the Land of Israel in the Jewish scheme of things.

As we celebrate, we are fully aware of all the problems and difficulties that confront the next decade. The 40 years have not brought a utopia. They tell us that we must continue to pray, to work, to act. Many years ago, the great poet Bialik, writing of the generation that left Egypt and marched toward the Promised Land, noted what we too must remember with sobriety: *Od haderekh rav, od rabbah hamilhamah.* "The way is yet great, the struggle is still mighty." Learning our sources should give us the strength and determination to cope!